Tuning t
STUDENT MIND

Tuning the
STUDENT MIND

A Journey in
Consciousness-Centered Education

Molly Beauregard

SUNY PRESS

Published by State University of New York Press, Albany

For information, contact State University of New York Press, Albany, NY
www.sunypress.edu

Library of Congress Cataloging-in-Publication Data

Names: Beauregard, Molly, 1965– author.
Title: Tuning the student mind : a journey in consciousness-centered
    education / Molly Beauregard.
Description: Albany : State University of New York, [2020] | Includes
    bibliographical references.
Identifiers: LCCN 2019049130 (print) | LCCN 2019049131 (ebook) | ISBN
    9781438478838 (hardcover : alk. paper) | ISBN 9781438478845 (pbk. : alk. paper)
    | ISBN 9781438478852 (ebook)
Subjects: LCSH: Affective education—United States. | Self-consciousness
    (Awareness)—Study and teaching (Higher)—United States. | College
    students—United States—Psychology. | Education, Higher—Aims and
    objectives—United States.
Classification: LCC LB1072 .B48 2020 (print) | LCC LB1072 (ebook) | DDC
    370.15/34—dc23
LC record available at https://lccn.loc.gov/2019049130
LC ebook record available at https://lccn.loc.gov/2019049131

10 9 8 7 6 5 4 3 2 1

Contents

Acknowledgments

I would like to extend my deepest gratitude to those whose teaching, friendship, and encouragement have contributed to the writing of this book. While countless individuals have influenced this work, there are a few standout, shining stars without whom this work would not have seen the light of day.

A huge, heartfelt thank you to Deborah Steinberg for helping me to transform a ragtag collection of blog posts, lecture notes, and short stories into an academic book that makes sense. I literally could not have done it without you.

Thank you to Rebecca Colesworthy and SUNY Press for taking a chance on an adjunct professor and first-time author. I am abundantly grateful for the opportunity to publish my book with you.

Warm appreciation to the College for Creative Studies for offering me the space to do my thing.

Appreciation to Elizabeth McQuillen and Emily Birchfield Shakibnia for their help with data analysis and research expertise.

Thank you to all the meditation teachers who have worked with my students over the years—most especially Jenny Barrett and Tim McMahon.

To the thousands of students who have walked through my classroom, I humbly bow to you. Thank you for showing up, for being curious, for being unique and special and crazy and wise and utterly untamable. You have brought me immeasurable pleasure, tremendous learning, and too many laughs. I am forever humbled by the honor of being your teacher.

Thank you to all the friends and colleagues who have listened to me whine, pontificate, and wax poetic about my book writing efforts. Special shout-out to my book club, Val Weiss, Ed Sarath, Mark Taylor, Mark Wiskup, Michael Stone-Richards, Caitlin Boyle, Mary Waldon, Mary McNichols, Deb Smith, and the magical, irreplaceable Gil Younger.

Thank you to my wonderfully supportive family—especially my mother, who first introduced me to Transcendental Meditation almost thirty years ago.

This book would not have happened without the support, friendship, and incredible vision of Chelsea Jackson. I am forever in your debt. Thank you.

And, finally, thank you Maddy, Cami, Charlie, and Mike—you are the great loves that sustain and inspire me every day and every way. Love you to the moon and back times infinity.

Note on the Text

The conversations recounted in this book all come from personal recollection. While these interactions are not written to reflect exactitude, I've done my best to adhere to the integrity of memory. In order to maintain student anonymity, I have changed the names of individual students as well other identifying features related in their work. In some cases, small edits—mostly grammatical and occasionally for the purpose of flow—have been made to student papers. My intention in sharing student writing is to showcase the powerful reflections elicited by the experience of consciousness-centered education.

In addition to a full bibliography, I include an annotated list of recommendations for further reading. These recommendations, all of which appear in the full bibliography as well, form the basis of the core curriculum for my course.

This book is story based, though I have also included a research appendix. There you will find a compilation of data and analysis from over seven years of student survey responses. My goal in offering this more academically traditional template of evidence is to shine a light on the potential impact of consciousness-centered education initiatives.

Introduction

An Angel Museum

Don't just teach because that's all you can do. Teach because it's your calling. And once you realize that, you have a responsibility to the young people.

—Maya Angelou

The first story I share every semester in my sociology class, Consciousness, Creativity, and Identity, is the real-life history of the Angel Museum.

It all began in 1976, when Joyce and Lowell Berg were vacationing in Florida. They happened to stop at an antique shop, where they fell in love with an Italian bisque figurine of two angels on a seesaw. They immediately bought it and brought it back home to Beloit, Wisconsin, where it became the first cherished artifact in what would eventually become a very grand collection of angels.

With my students, I usually take some creative liberties with my story about the humble beginnings of the Angel Museum. I imagine Joyce and Lowell scouring the world for angel imagery—passionate in their obsession and abundantly inclusive. I know for a fact that they find angel imagery at rummage sales. They save plastic angels that come on the tops of cakes (with the frosting still encrusted on the bottom). They hunt down angels at craft shows and antique fairs. They look for angels in shops and in garages, and they happily embrace every angel they find.

I imagine Lowell coming home from work one day and exclaiming to Joyce, "I can't live like this anymore! The angels are taking over our home!" There are angels on the wallpaper and on the countertop, rows of angels in special handmade cabinets, and punch-out windows with angels dangling from fishing wire. Joyce, of course, sees her cherished angels as art; she knows her collection is worthy of a great museum. She envisions herself as the caretaker of the angels. Her passion is so great and her heart so generous, she dreams of sharing her love of angels with the people of Beloit.

Joyce and Lowell begin their search for a new angel home in earnest. At first, there are some who doubt them—people who wonder if the world really needs an angel museum (especially one that includes "dollar-store special" angels stamped *Made in China*). But Joyce and Lowell prevail. Eventually, they find an old church building to lease. They load up a truck, and they set up shop. The angels are reframed, cleaned, put behind glass. Bright lights highlight the shining stars, and a small gift shop graces the lobby.

I imagine the first days as quiet—Joyce in her angel costume at the front door, Lowell wringing his hands over slow ticket sales, a trickle of friends wandering about admiring the eclectic and somehow strangely inspiring collection of angels. And then, suddenly (I pause here when I am speaking for an especially dramatic punch) . . . Oprah! Oprah hears about the Angel Museum and donates her collection of more than six hundred Black angels. Now, busloads of visitors arrive from across the Midwest to share in Joyce and Lowell's dream. The Angel Museum is a legitimate tourist attraction.

I share this story with my students for many reasons. On the surface, the Angel Museum story offers them an example of the infectious power of a shared dream and an allegory for how we construct meaning as a culture. It illustrates a central theme in the academic field of sociology: that meaning is created, not inherent or fixed. I share with my students my guess that the Bergs' angel collection grew innocently and organically. The angel from the top of the cake was licked clean of frosting and placed on the shelf above the kitchen sink. Years later, when placed under glass and lit from behind, it resonated in a completely new way. The collection gained status when it moved from the Berg home to a museum building. And it gained prestige when the powers that be, including Oprah, the local press, and funders, celebrated its worth. What was once considered kitsch became museum-worthy art under the loving gaze of the Bergs.

I also share this story with my students because it's a powerful metaphor for the creation of my class, SOC 322: Consciousness, Creativity, and Identity.

⌒〜

When I tell people that I teach at an art and design school, they immediately assume that I am a working artist. I never dispute their assumption. While I teach sociology, I view my work as art. I envision culture as a tapestry of sorts—understanding how it is woven together allows us to see the ways our life patterns are entrenched in our society. As Ralph Waldo Emerson wrote, "But relations and connection are not somewhere and sometimes, but everywhere and always."[1] What excites me about sociology is that by investigating these connections, we begin to understand how we fit in—or don't fit in—with our culture, and by understanding how we are connected, we gain the power to more clearly feel and grow empathy for ourselves and others.

Being a student of cultural patterns for most of my life has convinced me of one basic truth: compassion is the source of human happiness. We see this in personal relationships, in community initiatives, and in every sphere of public and private life. Where there is compassionate action there is social justice, where there are compassionate relationships there are healthy families, and when we suffer collectively from natural disasters or national tragedy we seek compassionate leadership. Compassion and loving-kindness serve as the root source of the best aspects of our human culture. And where these qualities are absent, we suffer in lonely despair and darkness.

Compassion serves as the golden thread that runs through the cultural tapestry I envision. As a sociology teacher working at an art and design school, I became obsessed with weaving this gold thread through my classroom. I asked myself repeatedly: Is the way that I am teaching sociology inspiring my students to understand their interconnection to each other and the broader world? Do these art students, who work so brilliantly with their hands and eyes, recognize that their lives are equally important works of art? Using the theme of compassion for oneself and others, I began to wonder what would happen if I tried to weave together three separate strands of influence into a single braid in my classroom. How might I bring objectivity, subjectivity, and unity together in the classroom? And would an environment that included all three of these approaches to knowing produce a better student, a more compassionate citizen, a happier individual?

I set out to design and implement a class with the goal of exploring these questions. The process of designing the curriculum included three

---

1. Ralph Waldo Emerson, *The Spiritual Emerson* (London: Penguin, 2008), 184.

important components. First, a syllabus with the expected titles of a midlevel sociology class. Second, the creation of a unique research paper assignment: the self. And, third, the inclusion of a meditation practice to allow students to feel the unity that underlies all experience. Together, these three approaches cultivate the silence and self-awareness needed for true introspection and profound thought.

The class's academic subject matter has been developed around the idea of investigating the impact of contemporary culture on the development of personal identity. Sociologists have developed a multitude of ways to define different identities. These include our race, class, and gender as well as our role identity, social identity, and collective identity. Each of these identities is related to an individual's self-concept. We use these different identities to navigate the world, as they help us infer our similarities and differences with other people. But, how do we teach students to see and understand our connections and the sameness that underlies all our experience—our common humanity?

This question led naturally to the second component of my class: the self. In order to inspire my students to integrate the academic concepts in sociology with their subjective experience of themselves in the world, I challenge them to write a paper in which they explore the sociological concepts we study through the lens of several of their own life experiences. By applying critical analysis of the texts we study to their own lives and integrating both objective and subjective insight, these young people begin to discover the full potential of their minds. Moreover, instead of just a grade—a number or a letter—my students receive personal letters, letters from me to them. Following each assignment, and at the end of the course, each student receives a letter that offers not just guidance, critique, and reflections on their academic work, but mentorship, support—and yes, love—for them as students, as learners, and as individuals. (Here, I must offer the caveat that my approach to this class is linked to my broader mission to gain an understanding of the impact of consciousness-centered educational programs. I recognize fully that it would be difficult for most teachers to provide such time-intensive, tailored feedback to every student enrolled in their classes. This is not to suggest that the work done in other classrooms is less substantive: rather, it is an acknowledgement of the unique conditions of my situation.)

The third component of the class, meditation, required a bit more thought. In fact, I considered implementing several different meditation styles. It was important to me that my students be taught by professionally trained meditation teachers. My goal was to be able to measure the impact of the integration of the practice, so I wanted to approach the meditation from an evidence-based perspective. This process is more clearly outlined in chapter 2. In the end, I chose to include a mantra-based meditation practice. My own twenty-five year practice is rooted in this tradition. As a result, it seemed natural, and I felt the most prepared, to offer my students the same technique in class. Initially, my students learned Transcendental Meditation, and later Primordial Sound Meditation—both mantra-based practices.

Combining the objective process of intellectually questioning the boundaries of identity with the subjective experience of transcending those same boundaries offers students a unique opportunity. As the great sages of history suggest, when a person is able to transcend the experience of living as a finite self with a limited ego, they touch the universal spirit that connects us all to the eternal, unchanging, infinite unmanifest that pervades each and every one of us. This is the knowledge and the experience I seek to share with my students—that we have a "here and now" identity and a timeless connection to the infinite beyond.

By integrating the skills of introspection, silence, and reflection with intellectual engagement, I offer my students not only a formal introduction to the academic disciplines of sociology and identity studies, but a guided opportunity to learn for the sake of self-discovery. Throughout this book I refer to this model as consciousness-centered education.

When I first proposed the idea of integrating meditation into the core curriculum of my class, I was met with deep skepticism and resistance. The idea of sitting in silence seemed to threaten the idea of classrooms as active spaces designed for learning. Fortunately, things have changed significantly in higher education circles since then. As the growing body of research on the benefits of mindfulness and meditation has evolved, educators have become significantly more open to the idea of integrating silence into the classroom. There are programs designed specifically to reduce delinquency, improve test scores, and enhance creativity. While 2009 marked the first annual conference of the Center for Contemplative Mind in Society at Amherst, today that same organization sponsors dozens of webinars, conferences, and training retreats.

Part of the pleasure of developing this course stems from the excitement of being part of a new wave of innovative initiatives in the academy. Driven, in large part, from an increased understanding of brain science, meditation in education is undergoing a renaissance of sorts. Recent research in the field of neuroscience offers evidence that "every sustained activity ever mapped—including physical activities, sensory activities, learning, thinking, and imagining—changes the brain as well as the mind."[2] We now know that the brain we were born with changes over time and is influenced both by experience and practical exercises, including mindfulness exercises and meditation. The research is conclusive: We can rewire our brains to think and feel differently. As a result of this new information, contemplative pedagogies in the classroom are viewed with less skepticism and often as a vehicle for transformational growth.

And over the last decade, my class has become one of the most popular offerings at the College of Creative Studies (CCS) in Detroit and was the subject of a short documentary film, *Tuning the Student Mind*, from which this book takes its title. Directed by my former student, Chelsea Richer (who now goes by her married name, Chelsea Jackson), the film shares the transformational journey of three students enrolled in my class. In addition to being nominated for a Social Impact Media Award, the film aired on Detroit Public Television and at the Freep Film Festival. Since then, I have enjoyed the opportunity to share the film with hundreds of college students and faculty members on college campuses across the country. During follow-up conversations and correspondence with teachers, students, and higher educational administrators, it has become obvious to me that there exists a sincere interest to learn more about the content and structure of my class.

This book shares my own story of working to create opportunities for students to look deeply into their own personal development and life as a part of the interconnected web of human experience. I invite you to join my students and me as we journey together through the class, exploring issues of identity, consciousness, and creativity at the individual, communal, and global levels. Each chapter in this book covers a week of the class and focuses on a different concept in the sociology of identity studies. I share some of the stories and activities I use to teach this material, as well as the pedagogical theories behind consciousness-centered education. I also include personal stories from my own journey that highlight how

---

2. Norman Doidge, *The Brain Changes Itself: Stories of Personal Triumph from the Frontiers of Brain Science* (London: Penguin, 2007), 288.

the teacher-student relationship is one of reciprocal learning. Each chapter concludes with an excerpt from a student paper discussing how the sociological concept discussed in the chapter applies to his or her own life. It is followed by an excerpt from my personal response to the student's paper.

Choosing the papers that are included in the book was an intuitive process—frankly, the papers that ended up in the book were some of the best written, most heartfelt, and most obviously related to the themes discussed in class. In short, I felt that these papers revealed awakenings—qualitative evidence that students gain a new way of seeing the self as related to culture, family, and past events in my class. These excerpts of student work and teacher responses illustrate how consciousness-centered education transforms and enriches the student-teacher relationship.

In creating a new type of college course, I did not at first intend to radically disrupt the usual student-teacher relationship. But in reflection on a decade of the practice, I see that my students and I have done just that. My attempt to engage the whole being in the educational process forces me to move beyond intellectual discourse. It forces my students and me to engage emotionally, spiritually, and ethically.

As a result, this book is deliberately personal and subjective, because it makes the case for bringing these qualities into the classroom and highlights, through its form as a personal memoir, that there are levels of understanding that cannot be accessed by objective accounts alone. It is not intended as a comprehensive overview or an objective defense of contemplative practices in education. Rather, it is essentially a teaching memoir that offers one subjective account of incorporating meditation practices and subjective reflection into a higher education course.

It is my hope that my story will resonate with professors working in contemplative studies and education departments at the college level. I also see this book serving as a resource to teachers in training who may consider incorporating meditation practices into their future courses. But, if truth be told, it is my most fervent hope that this book appeals to college students who may see themselves in the shared stories of their peers and feel inspired to know that there is a viable pathway to expanding their sense of self and their educational experience.

When I first started designing my class, people looked at me sideways. Similar to Joyce with her collection of angels, I was that eccentric lady with a weird hobby she can't shut up about. Slowly, with persistence and consistency, I have proven to my institution and administrators that this model for education is transformative. Student feedback, research evidence, and institutional support are the legitimizing forces that validate my model. This book is a guided tour of my museum.

First Week

Why Do You Believe
What You Believe about Yourself?

Man does not simply exist but always decides what his existence will be, what he will become the next moment. By the same token, every human being has the freedom to change at any instant.

—Viktor E. Frankl

Taking Off the Velcro Suit and Shock Collar

Long before I attended graduate school in sociology, I nurtured a bit of an obsession with cultural patterns. Why do people believe what they do about the world around them? Are things the way they are because they must be? Or, is it possible that a different cultural pattern might take hold in a society that interacted in a different way?

The truth is, these are big ideas. And, while easy to understand at the superficial level, the implications are pretty complicated. One of my teaching goals is to encourage students to "live" the knowledge. What I mean by "living the knowledge" is to take these theoretical and abstract ideas and apply them meaningfully to personal, subjective experiences. I do this through a series of in-class exercises.

It is typically the first week of class that I ask students to imagine that every morning, in addition to brushing their teeth, checking their phones, and drinking coffee, they also put on a full-body Velcro suit and an electric dog collar. They look at me like I am crazy. What's the point of this exercise? The point is to start thinking about the impact of interaction without awareness. Ideas stick to Velcro. You risk getting shocked if you cross a boundary while wearing an electric collar. At the end of every day, you come home with a whole bunch of expectations, ideologies, and generally crazy ideas about what it means to be successful, what it means to be happy, and what it means to be human. And, certainly, you will have neck burns if you happen to wear your shoes through security at the airport, reveal your political leanings to the wrong audience, or accidentally call "she" a "he."

Taking off the Velcro suit and dog collar can be an awfully humbling moment. For most students, this thought exercise provides a radical shift in understanding the ways identity is constructed via interactions and immersion in the cultural landscape. It helps students to recognize identity as a fluid tapestry rather than a hardened reality. Pretty quickly, everyone begins to acknowledge that they have learned what it means to be human—in all of its dimensions—through past interactions and social context.

Reality Is Socially Constructed

Sociologists stress that human knowledge of the world is socially constructed. In their classic book, *The Social Construction of Reality: A Treatise in the Sociology of Knowledge*, Peter Berger and Thomas Luckmann propose that language and systems of representation do not reflect an already existing reality so much as they organize, construct, and mediate the world around us. In other words, social order is a human product, or more precisely an ongoing human production.[1] If we accept this as a true statement, then we must also acknowledge that our view of the world is partial at best, limited by the cultural norms and expectations of the society in which we live. Think about this for a moment. Why do you believe what you believe about yourself, your family, and your community? We learn what it means to be human because of past interactions. Nothing has meaning in itself; it is the relationship of different concepts, contexts, and roles that generates meaning. Understanding is limited by one's evolving perspective.

---

1. Peter L. Berger and Thomas Luckmann, *The Social Construction of Reality: A Treatise in the Sociology of Knowledge* (New York: Anchor Books, 1966).

Additionally, and importantly, as the social theorist Michel Foucault suggested, we have systems in place that encourage us to self-regulate without the active threat of punishment. Individuals internalize the managerial gaze that watches over us. Think Orwellian Big Brother. The amorphous feeling that someone is watching our actions influences our behavior and thinking. This is a crucial component in the construction of our Velcro suits. It is also a not-so-subtle reference to the metaphorical electric dog collar. We maintain self-imposed control by internalizing expected boundaries.

Historically, the Velcro suit may not have posed much of an encumbrance. There were only so many roles a person could play in one lifetime. As a result, interaction and exposure to a diversity of ideas was limited. Read any great piece of historical literature and you will quickly remember how squeezed most individuals felt by the narrow parameters of identity. Think Emma Bovary, the Invisible Man, Anna Karenina. Rigid expectations tied to specific roles defined previous generations. "I am Dad. I am breadwinner. I am worker. I know who I am!" There is no doubt that these clear-cut patterns of identity development left scars of their own. But, I wonder how many college students today relate to the impossible squeezes faced by previous generations? For most of us, the identity squeeze of the twenty-first century has a very different day-to-day reality.

Identity refers to an individual's place in organized social life. It is a crucial aspect of self. Our identity may be situated, social, or personal. In other words, it is related to the roles we play, the way we identify with belief systems, and, most importantly, our internal recognition of our integrated sense of self. My experience working with young people has exposed a vulnerability in this third aspect of identity development. Young people seem to be cognizant of the roles they play and the beliefs they hold, but few have established a recognizable internal sense of self. They are, as a result, overly influenced by their identification with others.

It's hard changing your perception of yourself when you don't know who you are in the first place. Individuals who don't have a clearly developed sense of self allow the environment to have an undue influence on their identities. The focus this first week in class is to emphasize the following point: if you don't know yourself, your identity is left to be interrupted and created by your surroundings and the individuals around you. The issue is that in the bombardment of the visual landscape, the noise of the modern age, and the competitive frenzy to stay ahead of the game, most of us simply stay at the very surface level of existence. We let the world tell us who we are and what we see rather than diving deep within ourselves and catching our own unique vision of our true potential.

Our personal lives are the expression of our inner potentialities. Teaching students how to access this inner knowingness profoundly reshapes student experience and, by extension, the educational landscape. Individuals generally see a change of consciousness as a challenge to identity. Sociologists and psychologists have narrowly defined attributes of identity and how they relate to behavior, to mental health, and to belief systems. We become our beliefs, our diagnoses, our histories, our jobs, and our choices. Through these frameworks of definitions, we understand ourselves to be splintered aspects of a whole. Rather than acknowledging the mystery of the underpinnings of identity, we measure momentary expressions and behaviors of individuals. These narrow definitions of understanding do not capture the essence of identity any more than one photo tells the story of an entire life. Sadly, they also ignore the question of what an individual can become.

From Apathy to Engagement

In my classroom incubator, I have found that teaching young people to access their internal sense of being via meditation transforms their sense of self as well as their aptitude for learning. This happens when we incorporate subjective methodologies back into the classroom. I have also found that in addition to sharing knowledge, sharing my own reflections from mothering and living enriches the classroom environment.

Sometimes I wonder whether it is appropriate to engage in personal conversation with students. I am not a trained psychologist, and policies within higher education encourage referral to wellness centers for students suffering from mental health challenges. That said, ignoring the very real suffering that I see in my classroom presents an ongoing challenge. Does one ignore the cries of young people seeking comfort? Faculty meetings reveal a real frustration with what many teachers perceive to be the failings of their students. Rarely do I hear educators question the issues embedded in the educational process or shifts in the current cultural climate that contribute to the high levels of anxiety, depression, and other stress-related illnesses seen in students today.

I began to notice a shift in my classroom in 2007. It was becoming increasingly difficult to connect with my students. Sometimes I felt like a dog and pony show, working for scraps that came in the form of an interesting question or a shy smile from my audience. For the first time in my teaching career, I found myself struggling to engage my students with the material I found so fascinating. Selfishly, I wanted them to care about the issues that had inspired me years earlier during my own college experience. Truth be told, I couldn't find a student activist on campus to save my life. I would share stories of my own engagement with social justice issues at the University of Michigan, and they would look at me like I was speaking Greek. To be honest, my initial response to their lack of interest was frustration, but over time I found myself feeling for these numbed-out, disengaged, sad-feeling kids who kept showing up in my classroom. They didn't seem to have the energy to be interested in much other than making it from Monday to Tuesday.

One of my first responses to this changing atmosphere was to institute my "no phones or computers in the classroom" rule. I told my students they could take notes on paper or just sit and listen, but no more hiding behind screens in my classroom. The rule came after I had dramatically walked to the back of the classroom to make a point only to turn around and see dozens of open computers filled with gaming and Facebook imagery. I had mistakenly assumed that the tapping sounds of keyboards was due to thorough note-taking.

And then there was the spattering of quiet confessions offered at the end of class or during office hours. In hushed voices, thoughtful and often anguished students shared their personal sorrows with me. Several confided in me that they had made serious attempts on their lives during high school. Meanwhile, more and more notices were coming from the student success center about learning disabilities and mental health diagnoses. When I find myself thinking about that time, I feel the heaviness of a deep-seated sorrow.

My observations were validated during a faculty meeting called by the head of our student success center in 2008. My fellow faculty members and I learned that the center had been beleaguered by upset, burned-out students all year. According to the director, the behavior of our students mirrored what she was hearing from other professionals in learning centers across the country. Counseling and mental health support centers nationwide were seeing epidemic rates of student stress.

What she saw was the fallout from a culture that bombards all of us—and particularly young people—with an overload of visual and sensory stimuli. For students, who often also face an educational climate that places them under enormous pressure to achieve and produce, this culture can be particularly toxic. In addition to lacking inspiration, college students report anxiety disorders, drug abuse, and compromised academic performance. And it's getting worse. In 2014, the University of California, Los Angeles, Cooperative Institutional Research Program's annual survey revealed that entering first-year college students had reported the lowest levels of self-rated emotional health since the survey began forty-nine years ago.[2]

In cases where students come to school already suffering from underlying disorders such as Attention Deficit Disorder (ADD), Attention Deficit Hyperactivity Disorder (ADHD), and bipolar disorder, symptoms of anxiety, depression, and academic disengagement are often magnified. For a minority of students, the symptoms are truly extreme. Between 6.6 and 7.5 percent of undergraduate students report having seriously considered suicide.[3] And 19 percent of college students aged eighteen to twenty-four meet the criteria for an alcohol use disorder, yet don't seek treatment.[4]

But even students who otherwise present as healthy, productive, and engaged often report feeling overwhelmed and emotionally unmoored—and, ultimately, ill-prepared to learn. It's clear that the most stressed minority of students represents the tip of the iceberg, distracting us from the broad majority of college-age students whose emotional health is in jeopardy.

Surely, a multitude of cultural factors contribute to emotional distress among college-age adults. Researchers report that the rise in social media use and the decline of real-time socializing may be among them.

---

2. K. Eagan, E. B. Stolzenberg, J. J. Ramirez, M. C. Aragon, R. S. Suchard, and S. Hurtado, "The American Freshman: National Norms Fall 2014," *Higher Education Research Institute* (2015), http://www.heri. ucla.edu/tfsPublications.php.

3. Number ranges reflect research from multiple sources: M. D. Hanover, "American College Health Association–National College Health Assessment II: Undergraduate Reference Group Executive Summary Spring 2012," American College Health Association, 2012, http://www. acha-ncha.org/docs/ACHA-NCHA-II_UNDERGRAD_ReferenceGroup_ExecutiveSummary_Spring2012.pdf; "Healthy Minds Study," Healthy Minds Network, Ann Arbor: University of Michigan, 2012, http://www.healthyminds network.org; Substance Abuse and Mental Health Services Administration, Center for Behavioral Health Statistics and Quality, "Results from the 2012 National Survey on Drug Use and Health (NSDUH): Mental Health Detailed Tables," 2013, http:// www.samhsa.gov/data/NSDUH/2k12MH_FindingsandDetTables/MHDT/NSDUH MHDetTabsLOTSect1pe2012.htm.

4. L. T. Wu, D. J. Pilowsky, W. E. Schlenger, and D. Hasin, "Alcohol Use Disorders and the Use of Treatment Services among College-Age Young Adults," *Psychiatric Services* 58, no. 2 (February 2007): 192–200, http://www.ncbi.nlm.nih.gov/pubmed/17287375.

Constant digital connectedness and social pressure to perform may be others. But the lack of time and space to reflect, look inward, and find moments to detach from and transcend the constant pulse of input are important additional factors.[5]

That faculty meeting forced me to more carefully consider the suffering I saw in my own students. It led me to notice big patterns in the small data points I observed in my classroom each semester. I remembered that the semester before, during a media studies course I was teaching, a student had stopped me midstream and said, "Molly, I just feel so overwhelmed by the enormity of the problems I see in the world. It's so depressing and so impossible to imagine my personal ability to impact change anywhere." His sincerity silenced the room. Emboldened, I tossed my organized syllabus in the trash and totally revamped the semester's learning objectives. By the end of the course, a cohort of students within my class had raised $5,000 by designing and implementing an entire "Who Cares?" media campaign dedicated to supporting Habitat for Humanity programs in Detroit. It was a small step, but an important development in my work as an educator. I had witnessed the most disgruntled and disengaged students in my course transform their attitudes with a simple shift in focus: away from *measurement*, and toward *meaning*.

The following year, I unveiled a new course, with meditation—and a quest for meaning—at the center. Writing was pivotal to this quest. Throughout the semester, students were required to maintain a journal, write a critical essay, and, as their final assignment, submit a research paper that examines personal identity within the cultural context. This first paper, written by a graduating senior, feels especially poignant to me. Becky's story is one that I find increasing common amongst my students: the way a diagnosis becomes integral to the understanding of personal identity.

Student Paper: Becky—"Mental Illness and Me"

My clearest memory is standing at the front door begging my mom not to leave. I was seven years old. This defining moment marked the beginning of an emotionally unstable life. Prior to my parents' divorce, my mom

---

5. Tyler Kinkaid, "College Freshmen Are More Depressed and Alone Than Ever," *Huffington Post*, February 5, 2015, http://www.huffingtonpost.com/2015/02/05/college-students-depressed-ucla_n_6624012.html.

and I were together every day. And, then we just weren't—ever again. I was heartbroken without explanation.

My dad struggled to raise three girls on his own. He mostly did a pretty good job. But, in order to keep a roof over our head, he had to work two—sometimes three—jobs. So, you can imagine, he was fairly distracted much of the time. I just ached for my mom. It was especially bad at night. I missed my mom so much I couldn't sleep. I also started worrying about her. My dad eventually bought me one of those little flip phones that held like two or three numbers. He even bought me this little rainbow-colored zip-up purse to keep the phone protected. I slept with that phone. Every night I texted my mom as soon as I got in bed. Some nights, she texted right back. But, lots of nights, I wouldn't hear from her. I slept with that phone next to my head for years—always in anxious anticipation for word from my mom.

I remember that it was about this same time that I became more aware of the dangers in the world. Every night I feared going to sleep without talking to my mom. I would lie in bed thinking, "What if she's in danger? Maybe she's not answering because she needs help?" For two years, I slept with that small purse containing my cell phone and some spare change. I was always "at the ready" in case I ever had to jump into action to save her. I worried about my mom a lot—our broken communication always kept me on edge.

I became a lazy kid. I never did my homework. Sometimes I would start homework, but my efforts would trail off as soon as I got stumped or bored. I idolized my older sisters. I never wanted to ask for help, as I feared they would think I was dumb or, worse, annoying. My attention span mimicked that of a goldfish. My inability to get my homework completed did not stem from a blatant disregard for school. The ten year old who didn't have anyone to tell her to do her homework evolved into a monster that survived by doing homework while it was being collected. I fell into a cycle that I couldn't seem to shift no matter how hard I tried. Looking back now, I realize I more than likely needed a tutor, but what I got was a prescription.

Between my mom and dad, I grew up adopting unhealthy coping mechanisms. My dad often responded to stress with anger and aggression, while my mom tended to cry and shut down. There were never any discussions on mental health or illness or coping skills in my home setting, or in my school for that matter. After being analyzed for what felt like forever, I was officially diagnosed with ADHD and given an Adderall prescription to help me focus in school. I struggled to take it for the first year. It was helpful during the day. I managed to stay engaged in class, be less disruptive, and more productive. But, as soon as 2:30 p.m. hit, I would get angry about anything and everything. I started to accept that I had a broken brain. Sure, I was a mindless zombie with a short temper, but I was doing my homework, and that's what everyone seemed to care about.

Fast forward to college. I chose to attend art school because I naïvely believed it would offer me release from academic stress. However, my childhood patterns of poor time management and homework neglect caught up to me fast. Each semester I lost sleep doing last-minute work and stressing about details. By the end of each semester I felt panicked. I tended to lash out at others, experience crying jags, and be aggressive with friends and family. Adding fuel to the fire, I had foot surgery the summer after freshman year. It was an excruciating recovery filled with Percocet and depression. I ended up taking pain relievers for five months. When I finally stopped taking them, I fell into a six-month depression that caused me to continually lash out at others, contemplate suicide, and, more than anything, recognize and feel the depth of my anxiety. In the midst of the worst stress, my body would tremble and go numb. My thoughts raced out of control and my tears didn't stop. It was literally terrifying.

The trauma of this time eventually—thankfully—led me to therapy. While I am still a work in progress, I am beginning to connect the dots between my early experiences as a child, the cultural landscape, and my own journey into mental illness. Sometimes, I wonder about the impact of sleeping with that phone next to my head. It's silly, I know, but I can't help but wonder about the impact of those electromagnetic waves. Writing this paper offered me the opportunity to piece together the interactional dynamics that helped construct my identity. It also helped me to recognize—for the first time—all the ways that societal norms influenced the ways people responded to my upset energy.

Dear Becky—

After a trauma, individuals process the events that happened to them. Sometimes this happens through the process of constantly thinking about what happened—and often with strong emotional reactions. The pain of missing your mom and feeling the

confusion in your family life as a young girl would naturally
elicit all kinds of upsetting feelings. Feeling hurt, vulnerable,
anxious, and scared are normal, healthy reactions to being deeply
traumatized. I am glad your work with a counselor is helping you
to recognize this truth.

Thinking of seven-year-old Becky makes me smile. However,
it squeezes my heart to imagine how tired you must have been.
Did you know that children and adults behave differently as
a result of sleepiness? Adults tend to become sluggish, while
children become hyperactive and inattentive. I recently read an
article linking sleep disorders to ADHD diagnoses. I encourage
you to spend a bit of time investigating this link as you finish up
your paper. A tired child in the classroom is a pain in the neck
for an overworked teacher. You likely got tagged as "problematic"
early, which likely led to your feelings that you had a "broken
brain." In his book *Super Brain*, Deepak Chopra writes, "The first
rule of super brain is that your brain is always eavesdropping
on your thoughts. As it listens, it learns. If you teach it about
limitation, your brain will become limited."[6]

Nothing happens overnight. We create our own story lines
every day. Our internal landscapes are informed by our daily
interactions—feeling building upon feeling. Over time, our
notions about ourselves are pretty well defined, and our behavior
becomes an almost automatic process of confirming what it is we
believe to be true about ourselves. Working to change patterns
set in childhood can be tough business. I admire your strength of
character to really peel back the layers of self.

Why do we believe what we believe to be true about
ourselves? Too often, our perceptions are shaped by situations
beyond our control. Sometimes we cannot help but have our ears
open when others speak ill of us. This can hurt deeply. But, it
is important to question the stories we believe about ourselves.
I am struck by the title of your paper: "Mental Illness and Me."
Be careful not to cling too dearly to your diagnosis. It represents
only one aspect of who you are, not the totality of your essence.

---

6. Deepak Chopra and Rudolph E. Tanzi, *Super Brain: Unleashing the Explosive Power
of Your Mind to Maximize Health, Happiness, and Spiritual Well-Being* (Harmony
Books, 2012), 16.

As you finish up your paper, I encourage you to take a look at the work of Dr. Thomas Armstrong. In his groundbreaking book, *The Myth of the ADD Child*, Armstrong argues that many behaviors labeled as ADD or ADHD are simply a child's response to complex social, emotional, and educational influences.[7] Imagine if you had been sent to a "nap room" when you first exhibited signs of hyperactivity in the classroom. It's a somewhat counterintuitive response, but my hunch is that nap time would have eased your symptoms in real and meaningful ways. One of the other themes Armstrong emphasizes in his work is the negative impact of an ADD diagnosis. You touch on this in your paper with your reference to your "broken brain." It seems this diagnosis became the primary way you navigated your identity during your teenage years. As you begin to question your assumptions, I think it is important to understand the cultural context of your diagnosis. Embodying this diagnosis as a personal failure or biological defect ignores the very real connection to ways the educational system, your family, and your doctors may have misinterpreted your symptoms.

One of the reasons I include meditation training in this class is to help students grow their ability to witness without attachment. In other words, to allow your mind to transcend the experience of thinking and engage in the process of watching your life unfold organically and spontaneously. When this happens, you may begin to feel as if "Becky" is the star of a great show. You will see very clearly all the ways your life is connected to other people. Remember my Velcro suit and dog collar exercise from the first week? The continued practice of meditation will help you to shed that suit. What a freeing experience that will be for you!

You are more than the story you have been told. Peeling back the layers of how you got here seems to have offered you some understanding and forgiveness of yourself for your perceived shortcomings. This is good news, as NOW is the time to start piecing yourself back together. In my experience, the most compassionate people are often the ones who have known

---

7. Thomas Armstrong, *The Myth of the A.D.D. Child: 50 Ways to Improve Your Child's Behavior and Attention Span without Drugs, Labels, or Coercion* (New York: Plume, 1997).

disappointment and suffering. Living through tough times grows a certain understanding and compassion for others. You seem to hold a lovely sensitivity within you, Becky. It will serve you well throughout your life.

Love,

Molly

Second Week

What Types of Knowledge Do We Value?

I never made one of my discoveries through the process of rational thinking.

—Albert Einstein

Forgetting to Breathe

Imagine yourself in the midst of a busy afternoon. This probably isn't hard to do. After a hectic day at your job, you dash to your car and head to the market to grab some ingredients for a quick dinner. The grocery store is packed with people, and there are only two checkout lanes open. You stifle a sigh of frustration and, like everyone else in line, pull out your phone while you wait. The first image in your Instagram feed is a beautiful photo of a stream running through the woods; it looks so calm and peaceful and makes you long to be anywhere but this brightly lit market. Across the photo, in simple lettering, is written: *Just Breathe.* Wow! That is so insightful. It's too easy to forget the most basic things in life. Everyone you know could use that reminder. You immediately share the post, then shove your phone into your pocket because it's your turn to check out. By the time you're back behind the wheel and on your way home, you've forgotten all about the lovely image and the importance of breathing. Your busy day-to-day reality has squashed your access to the quiet required to actually feel the glory of your breath.

I like to use this parable to get my students thinking about how they absorb and share knowledge. They quickly recognize that popular culture is littered with tag lines intended to lead us to enlightenment: *Live in the moment. Don't be attached. Meditate. Just do you. You are who you choose to be.* Operating outside a broader understanding of an articulated spirituality or philosophy, these abstracted ideas become diluted and meaningless. Like signposts in a desert, they point in the right direction, but they leave us without any road to travel.

Similarly, academia—in fields as diverse as eco-philosophy, quantum mechanics, and biophysics—offers theoretical missives and evidence-based research regarding humanity's relationship to the cosmos. Science tells us that the universe was created in a moment—an explosion beyond the magnitude of our wildest imagination. Our personal connection to this epic flash is the mere fact of our existence—each of us literally "being" a spark of light that splintered off of this churning, magnificent whirlwind of energy. But the flatness and lack of personal relevance in how this knowledge is taught leaves many of us feeling disconnected from the knowledge and incapable of truly integrating the facts into our everyday, subjective life experience.

Remembering to Feel

Educational models today function using mechanistic mandates that emphasize skill building. We generally measure our students' learning and define their "progress" by results on tests and papers, class participation, and attendance. Numbers matter. There are a multitude of benefits to this model. However, our system is wildly out of balance. Our test-heavy, career-focused, outcome-oriented educational models have resulted in a profound loss of meaning for students. Learning for the sake of learning is invoked as an abstract concept, but it's not a goal institutions are truly set up to pursue practically with their students. By emphasizing results and performance, I believe educators too often deny the validity of process. As a result, we erode the sense of meaning and purpose that should drive all inquiry and investigation.

The idea of measurable learning outcomes has conditioned, if not totally determined, our way of thinking about education. Intellectual understanding is important. However, it is not the only pathway for knowledge. In truth, intellectual life is simply a thin layer of thinking activity that covers the enormity of our internal awareness. In the deeper, more self-reflective or subjective regions of knowing we are, at our very basis, connected to the totality of the universal consciousness.

Life is, literally, filled with abstractions—both universal and personal. What is needed are ways to make this reality relevant to personal, everyday life experiences. People want to experience the invisible force that underpins their waking experience of themselves. They know it is there—just out of reach, hiding in the open. It is found in the momentary glimpses of transcendence in daily life—getting lost in thought while walking in the woods, being swept up in the joy of playing the piano, forgetting oneself while engaged in driving. We live for these moments of inner peace and awareness when the stresses of daily life simply fall away, and our experience of deep connection to the world around us feels complete.

Can you imagine the impact of training individuals to systematically seek these moments of transcendence? How would the cumulative layers of such peace on a day-to-day basis transform individual lives?

Consciousness-centered educational models do just that, integrating subjective, individual awareness with objective ways of knowing, allowing heart and mind to work together for deeper understanding and creativity. Constraining the heart in preference for the mind denies our spontaneous growth and cuts us off from opportunities to make new connections and consider new knowledge from different perspectives. We too often push love and compassion out of the classroom, relegating them to our students' "personal lives"—as though those lives aren't part and parcel of their classroom experience (an attitude that is particularly ironic in a field like sociology, which is the study of social relationships).

Likewise, my "personal life" as a woman, a mother, an American, and so forth is part and parcel of my teaching practice. I have practiced meditation since 1994, and it has had a major impact on my understanding of myself and my relationship to the people, society, culture, and world around me. In conceiving of a new type of class, meditation presented itself as one simple tool I could offer my students to enhance their understanding of themselves and how they relate to their environment. I introduce my students to meditation during the second class session, bringing in professional meditation trainers to teach them.

To be clear: my course is not a course about meditation. But meditation is an integral tool I share with my students that deepens their learning practices and their relationships with themselves.

The Exploration of Consciousness in My Classroom

I often laugh with students at the beginning of the semester, acknowledging the challenges inherent in proclaiming to teach a class on consciousness. There is no doubt that it is an audacious goal. As the philosopher David Chalmers explains, there is the "hard problem" and the "easy problem" of consciousness. The "easy" problem (which still seems pretty hard to me!) is to understand how the brain processes information. The "hard" problem is to explain the existence of subjective experience. It seems that no matter how much we know about how the brain works, we still can't explain why some people like chocolate vs. vanilla ice cream.

Chipping away at the hard problem encourages a variety of approaches to the field of consciousness studies. There are thinkers who reduce consciousness to the electrochemical processes in the brain. Others claim consciousness is not reducible to these processes but still depends on a physical substrate. And still others flip the scenario and view consciousness as primary, a view that is coherent with many spiritual traditions. As Charles Whitehead writes in "Six Keynote Papers on Consciousness, "The challenge of consciousness is such that we cannot afford to ignore any potentially useful approach, and I propose social analysis."[1]

More recently, academics have been taking up the study of consciousness to investigate the power of the mind. In *Extraordinary Knowing: Science, Skepticism, and the Inexplicable Powers of the Human Mind*, Elizabeth Lloyd Mayer calls on academics to take more seriously evidence of the legitimacy of reflective, subjective ways of knowing.[2] Mayer echoes famed psychologist William James's call to "enlarge the scope of science to include the study of phenomena that are random, non-repeatable, and dependent on personal capacities and dispositions."[3] As Mayer writes, "If there's anything in anomalous mental capacities, the door has to stay open to these questions. If we don't investigate them seriously, a portion of our experience will remain walled off, never pushed to real consequence, never assessed in the ongoing context of life. To pursue the questions behind

---

1. Charles Whitehead, "Six Keynote Papers on Consciousness with Some Comments on Their Social Implications: TSC Conference, Hong Kong, 10–14 June 2009," *Journal of Consciousness Studies* 17 (2010).

2. Elizabeth Lloyd Mayer, *Extraordinary Knowing: Science, Skepticism, and the Inexplicable Powers of the Human Mind* (New York: Bantam Books, 2007).

3. Mayer, *Extraordinary Knowing*, 265.

extraordinary knowing is to pursue a complete and free articulation of what it is to be human."[4]

Intellectualizing around the idea of consciousness is important. A back-and-forth debate helps us refine our conception of this intangible force that underpins existence. That said, by their very nature, definitions "bind" understanding—any concept of consciousness is ultimately, at its root, a thought. In my class, we take the view that consciousness can be best understood through self-referential investigation. This is why exploring consciousness via meditation offers students the unique experiment of experiencing themselves as consciousness.

Over the years, two different types of meditation have been taught in my class: Primordial Sound Meditation (PSM) and Transcendental Meditation (TM). Both techniques come from the Vedic tradition, which is born out of an interpretation of the Vedas. Written in Vedic Sanskrit, the Vedas represent the most ancient scriptures of Hinduism. This spiritual wisdom emphasizes inner exploration of the unmanifest reality that is basis of all of life—in other words, consciousness.

Vedic meditation practices encourage the exploration of our essential nature: unbounded consciousness in its purest form. Mediation, in this tradition, is not about forcing the mind to quiet or choosing and observing thoughts, rather it's a process to rediscover the quiet that underlies the very existence of the self. As Maharishi Mahesh Yogi writes, "The field of that absolute wisdom is not outside of you. You have not to go out anywhere to acquire it. It is within you. You have only to be within yourself, 'possessed of the Self,' ever firm in the purity of your own Being."[5]

According to Vedic science, sound is the subtlest of our sense experiences, and thoughts are a subtle form of sound. In a mantra-based meditation—like PSM or TM—individuals use sound in the form of a mantra as a vehicle of the mind. Mantras have no specific meaning. They are simply sounds with vibrational qualities. As a result, effortlessly repeating a mantra naturally interrupts the flow of thoughts, allowing the mind to slowly drift into the more subtle, abstract regions of silence. When the mantra and thoughts disappear, the only thing left is pure consciousness. As the philosopher Ken Wilber writes, "We are the victims of an epidemic case of mistaken identity, with our Supreme Identity quietly but surely

---

4. Mayer, *Extraordinary Knowing*, 272.

5. Maharishi Mahesh Yogi, *Bhagavad-Gita: Chapter 7* (Vlodrop, Netherlands: Maharishi Vedic University, 2009), xiii.

awaiting discovery. And the mystics want nothing more than to have us awaken to who, or what, we really and eternally are *beneath or under or prior* to our pseudo-self. Thus, they ask us to cease identifying with this false self, to realize that whatever I can know, think or feel about myself cannot constitute my real Self."[6]

Studies have shown that meditation offers a successful model for improving students' mental health. Mindfulness, the practice of purposefully paying attention to the present moment in a nonjudgmental manner,[7] has been widely associated with an array of positive health outcomes, such as an improved ability to focus, improved emotional regulation, and a reduction in stress, anxiety, and depression.[8]

Mantra meditation[9] is associated with similar favorable health and academic outcomes, including decreased anxiety and depression and improved coping and academic performance.[10] Mantra meditation is

---

6. Ken Wilbur, *The Essential Ken Wilber: An Introductory Reader* (Boston: Shambhala, 1998), 25.

7. Jon Kabat-Zinn, *Full Catastrophe Living: Using the Wisdom of Your Body and Mind to Face Stress, Pain, and Illness* (New York: Delacourt Press, 2005).

8. B. Hölzel et al., "Mindfulness Practice Leads to Increases in Regional Brain Matter Density," *Psychiatry Research* 191, no. 1 (2011): 36–43, doi: 10.1016/j.psychresns. 2010.08.006; Jon Kabat-Zinn, L. Lipworth, and R. Burney, "The Clinical Use of Mindfulness Meditation for the Self-Regulation of Chronic Pain," *Journal of Behavioral Medicine* 8 (1985): 163–90; J. A. Astin, "Stress Reduction through Mindfulness Meditation: Effects on Psychological Symptomatology, Sense of Control, and Spiritual Experiences," *Psychotherapy and Psychosomatics* 66 (1997): 97–106; Vicky Y. Chang et al., "The Effects of a Mindfulness-Based Stress Reduction Program on Stress, Mindfulness Self-Efficacy, and Positive States of Mind," *Stress Health* 20 (2004): 141–47.

9. S. Trama and N. Cheema, "Transcendental Meditation: Nature and Perspectives," *Indian Journal of Health and Wellbeing* 7, no. 9 (2016): 928–33.

10. Stanford I. Nidich et al., "A Randomized Control Trial on Effects of the Transcendental Meditation Program on Blood Pressure, Psychological Distress, and Coping in Young Adults," *American Journal of Hypertension* 22, no. 12 (2009): 1326–31, doi:10.1038/ajh.2009.184; K. R. Eppley, A. I. Abrams, and J. Shear, "Differential Effects of Relaxation Techniques on Trait Anxiety: A Meta-Analysis," *Journal of Clinical Psychology* 45 (1989): 957–74; Robert W. Cranson et al., "Transcendental Meditation and Improved Performance on Intelligence-Related Measures: A Longitudinal Study," *Personality and Individual Differences* 12 (1991): 1105–1116; K. T. So and David W. Orme-Johnson, "Three Randomized Experiments on the Longitudinal Effects of the Transcendental Meditation Technique on Cognition," *Intelligence* 29 (2001): 419–40.

particularly well suited for use in college classrooms due to the reported ease of practice, calming effects, and enjoyment that students experience when practicing.[11]

When professor and students meditate together as a class throughout the semester, and students are encouraged to maintain and reflect on their meditation practice outside of the classroom, students more effectively engage with their coursework. Proper meditation practice fosters greater mental clarity and emotional regulation among participating students, resulting in an improved ability to perform well academically and an increase in community connections.[12] Ultimately, students are healthier, more connected, and better prepared to successfully graduate college.

Meditation opens students' hearts and minds to learning, allowing them access to modes of thought that lie outside of intellectual analysis. The pure, unencumbered awareness that is gained during meditation unlocks the grip of their beliefs, their inhibitions, their likes and dislikes, their approvals and disapprovals. It gives them much-needed moments of quiet, and those moments enhance and drive deeper questions and richer conversations.

Awakening to Wonder

I might never have developed a course whose goal is the integration of objective and subjective knowledge were it not for my own experience with my infant son, Charlie, whose early development defied logical explanation and resisted traditional medical diagnosis. Born with an underdeveloped metabolic system, Charlie came into the world as a mystery. His systems did not work in a coordinated matter. None of his symptoms—acidosis, low platelet count, and jaundice—added up to a clear diagnosis or prognosis from neonatal experts. He slept twenty-two hours a day, and when he woke, he lay limp in my arms, barely present to concerns of the world.

11. A. Burke, "Comparing Individual Preferences for Four Meditation Techniques: Zen, Vipassana (Mindfulness), Qigong, and Mantra," *EXPLORE* 8, no. 4 (2012): 237–42.

12. Paul Condon et al., "Meditation Increases Compassionate Responses to Suffering," *Association for Psychological Science* (2013): doi:10.1177/0956797613485603; D. Lim, P. Condon, and D. De Steno, "Mindfulness and Compassion: An Examination of Mechanism and Scalability," *PLoS ONE* 10, no. 2 (2015): doi:10.1371/journal.pone.0118221.

Doctors poked and prodded. They shook their heads in confusion. My husband and I wondered and worried. Specialists offered kind, soft words of support. We filled prescriptions. Nurses took his blood. We waited.

One day, after a long time of suspended anticipation, Charlie simply woke up. For six long months, my boy and I had sat and rocked together in a quiet void. When he awoke with a gummy grin to the noise of the world, I came up to the surface with him, excited to investigate our shared world with greater intensity and compassion than I had before. Our doctors couldn't explain Charlie's slow process of becoming alive—his second birth, at six months old. Indeed, some of them had expected him to die. I didn't know it then, but the mystery of his becoming would send me off on a journey of my own.

Simply put, the mystery of Charlie's illness and recovery taught me about the power of absolute love. Observing his weakened state of halfway-here, I had found it difficult to imagine the boy Charlie would become. Sitting in the insecure space of not knowing our imagined future together, my heart felt the first stirrings of unbounded love. My love for this child wasn't tied to the normal expectations of growth and development. It could not be diluted by experience or knowledge. It simply was.

As a teacher, I wondered in the years after Charlie's illness whether I could create a learning environment that mirrored the atmosphere surrounding my baby's healing. We have been conditioned for a long time to accept the prevailing idea that learning and knowing can be measured and standardized. There is no doubt that the achievements of the last century have been profound; many of them—for example, sending a man to the moon, developing a vaccine for polio—are directly related to our culture's emphasis on empirical inquiry and scientific rationality. In my own training in sociology, I was taught to look at observed evidence, data and facts, statistics and bell curves.

But my experience with Charlie led me to question what I thought I knew about learning, teaching, and investigating. During a follow-up appointment at the University of Michigan when Charlie was three years old, the attending physician said to me, "Mrs. Beauregard, we just have no way to explain why a child who presented at birth like your son continues to thrive and grow as he does." I was moved by this humble admission of surprise. The rigors of traditional medical training could not prepare this doctor for my son's experience, or for mine.

I began to wonder: What if we made room in the classroom for recognizing the mysterious, liminal, transcendent moments life offers us every day?

Student Paper:
Samantha—An Instantaneous Connection to the Entire Universe

I don't tell many people the following story because I think it's a little crazy and unbelievable, even to myself. Sometimes I even doubt that I actually experienced it, because I can hardly even describe it. I don't think I can ever come up with a suitable description to fully explain what it was, because I don't really know *what* it was, but I will try.

I was in my senior year of high school. I lived in a residential high school dorm with one other roommate. I clearly remember standing in front of our dank little sink about to brush my teeth, when I just sort of blinked and saw something out of the corner of my eye. I saw my environmental science class (of all things) all seated at our lab tables, but then I also saw it in relation to the whole country, and then in relation to the whole earth. This was by far one of the strangest experiences I've ever had. I guess it could probably be chalked up to my sleep–deprived, stretched-thin brain at the time (my high school was not for slackers), and maybe it was. But that doesn't diminish the fact that I felt like I had just seen the whole earth in relation to myself—and specifically in relation to my senior class—put in place in a matter-of-fact way. The whole vision couldn't have lasted more than one second.

Coming from a nonreligious family, this was by far the most spiritually connected I've ever felt to anything. I might venture to say that this was a glance into what Henryk Skolimowski describes as "our innermost intuition (where) we are individually united with this ultimate oneness for which there is not word." It definitely was almost an impossible feeling to describe. And it was like nothing I'd ever heard about, especially since I was never very spiritual before this random, transcendent moment. I actually tried to find out if other people had similar out-of-body experiences to make myself feel less like a crazy person. I eventually shared this strange vision with one of my friends, who immediately perked up and said, "I've had one of those!" Together, we somehow stumbled across Abraham Maslow's definition of peak experiences.[13] We were greatly comforted by the notion that the possibility of such bizarre happenings exists.

I think this experience affected me in a weird way. It wasn't imme-diate. I didn't suddenly change my life course because of it. It was simply

---

13. Abraham H. Maslow, Bertha G. Maslow, and Henry Geiger, *The Farthest Reaches of Human Nature* (London: Penguin/Arkana, 1993).

a transpersonal moment that made me feel a connectedness to the earth, even though I'm so small and so insignificant. I think this experience opened my mind. Specifically, it helped me not to take things too seriously sometimes. I feel like now, I am able to brush little things off more easily, although I've always been able to distance myself from things. This particular peak experience, however, let me brush off problems because I think I realized how silly it would be to get upset over small things.

I try to share my thinking with friends whenever I hear them struggle with an issue: don't fret over that quiz, buddy. It's just one quiz out of one class out of one year of high school out of all your preadult life. You'll be okay. I'm not entirely sure if this helps my friends, or if they find it annoying. But I know I feel infinitely better when I calm down and realize the relative importance of things that I stress over. Sometimes it's hard for me to step back and realize, but that single experience really illuminated this way of thinking to me. I still get upset over things, but the more I move through my world, the more I've started to take things as they are, accept situations, and just roll with it. I wish I could just impart that second-long experience to everyone, because internalizing that experience has led to me worrying a lot less about what people think of me. It's a large part of my approach to quelling stress.

Dear Samantha—

Somehow your paper got buried in my email. I just this "moment second" (as my niece Maggie likes to say) read it. Wow. It is a beautiful paper—full of wise insights and lovely reflections.

I totally understand the difficulty of sharing the "peak experience." Words will never be able to express the fullness of seeing yourself related to all of creation. Speaking is linear; by nature it puts all kinds of boundaries around ideas. Besides, sometimes when words fall off our tongue, we have the immediate awareness that we have chosen the wrong audience. In the end, the retelling feels like we are chipping away at our most basic internal truth and the preciousness of "owning" an experience.

That said, I am so happy you shared with me! I felt myself slowly fall into your vision—tucked away in my own kitchen chopping onions, listening to music, and enjoying my own little space. Perhaps the following quote will resonate: "Know that all of nature is but a magic theater, that the great mother is the master magician, and that this whole world is peopled by her many parts."[14]

Samantha, you say you are not religious/spiritual. I beg to disagree. The fact that people make assumptions about what a "spiritual" person looks like has always made me smile. You know, an infinity tattoo, dreadlocks, or a white turban can go a long way toward playing the part of "spiritual." In reality, that is just a sign that someone can read the cultural clues and put together a good costume. It's as difficult to truly convey inner spirituality through these stylistic trappings as it is to describe it in words. Personally, I think it is a lot smarter to sit back and silently take in everything that is going on around you. Silence has the capacity to give strength to your internal power. Silence is more than just "not talking" and observing; it is experiencing the most abstract aspects of yourself and pulling more and more of that inner awareness into your everyday, subjective life experience. For me, experiencing this silence is the grandest "religious" experience anyone can have, for it is in silence that we are prone to gather up the knowingness of the universe. Besides, if my experience in the classroom has taught me anything, it is that generally the quiet ones have the most to reveal.

Samantha, do not discount your own beautiful smallness. I once heard a lecture given by Maharishi Mahesh Yogi; in it he said something to this effect: "The life of the individual in its every thought, word, and action influences the entire field of the cosmos. Therefore, someone with peace at heart naturally vibrates peace and harmony to influence the whole universe." The internal peace you describe so perfectly radiates out into the world seamlessly. While you may feel small from time to time, your nature supports all of us in real and tangible ways.

It has been a real pleasure to get to know you this past semester. You did a great job on this rough draft. Add citations

---

14. *The Upanishads*, trans. Alistair Shearer and Peter Russel (Emeryville, CA: Potter/TenSpeed/Harmony, 2010), 162.

for the references you mention in the draft, and you will be home free.

I look forward to watching your journey continue to unfold. I think you have much to look forward to.

Much love,

Molly

Third Week

What Does the American Dream Look Like Today?

The American dream is often a very private dream of being the star, the uniquely successful and admirable one, and the one who stands out from the crowd of ordinary folk who don't know how. And since we have believed in that dream for a long time and worked very hard to make it come true, it is hard for us to give it up, even though it contradicts another dream that we have—that of living in a society that would really be worth living in.

—Robert N. Bellah

Too Many Shades of Blue

You wake up on a Saturday morning enthusiastic about engaging in a little painting project. You are going to paint your bathroom blue! Upon arriving at Home Depot, you eagerly seek out an orange-aproned staffer capable of directing you to the paint department. While walking to aisle four, you discuss your plans with a certain gleeful excitement, describing in detail the blue walls that will match the small soap dish you bought in Mexico last year on spring break. Suddenly, the moment of truth arrives. The friendly staffer has directed you to an enormous, three-story-high wall of paint—blue paint, two thousand shades, to be exact. Shuffling out of Home Depot an hour and a half later, empty handed and defeated by your inability to choose the "right" blue, you stop to eat a hot dog at the cart in the entrance. Later, at home in bed—feeling slightly unhealthy, unproductive, and disoriented—you bemoan your inability to get anything done, ever.

The world in which we live will not let us rest. It distracts us and pulls at us and offers us endless choices of who we can be, what we can do, and how we can feel. Navigating this landscape is difficult—and at times, downright impossible. It leaves many young people feeling particularly vulnerable and overwhelmed, with no sense of how anything they do could matter much.

A big part of our mission as educators should be to help students understand why the liberal arts are relevant beyond the teaching of skills. We should be teaching our students what it means to be a good and thoughtful citizen of the world. The first and most natural step in this process is to encourage self-reflection in the classroom. Ultimately, this practice will help students become clear about what is most deeply meaningful to them. In other words, it will help them have the confidence to commit to a particular shade of blue in the face of a sea of blues.

American Individualism

Over the years, I have played around with the structure of my syllabi. In the end, however, I always return to the tried and true sociological classics. One of my personal favorites remains *Habits of the Heart: Individualism and Commitment in American Life*.[1] Published in 1989, *Habits* seeks to discover whether or not the virtue necessary for freedom and happiness is now being developed in American society. (Now, the word "virtue" can get a group of college kids feeling pretty defensive right off the bat. Right up front, I have to say, "Look, we are sticking to the lofty, 'golden rule' kind of virtue stuff. No talk of chastity belts or human sexuality." You need to disarm the conversation, you might say.) The book explores what resources Americans have for making sense of their lives, how individuals think about themselves and their society, and how people's ideas relate to their actions. The research—based on a large, five-year study of various American communities—concludes that we do not have a language that supports the development of virtue in American society. The authors argue that we have failed to remember "our community as members of the

---

1. Robert N. Bellah, Richard Madsen, William M. Sullivan, Ann Swindler, and Steven M. Tipton, *Habits of the Heart: Individualism and Commitment in American Life* (Berkeley: University of California Press, 1985).

same body."[2] In fact, they believe we have committed what the republican founders of our nation considered the cardinal sin: we have put our own good, as individuals, as groups, as a nation, ahead of the common good.

The title *Habits of the Heart* comes from French social philosopher Alexis de Tocqueville. Tocqueville, who traveled throughout the United States for a year in the 1830s, described the mores of this country as "habits of the heart."[3] He singled out family life, religious traditions, and participation in local politics as helping to create the kind of person who could sustain a connection to a wider political community and thus ultimately support the maintenance of free institutions. He believed the key to the survival of free institutions was the relationship between public and private life—the ways citizens do, or do not, participate in the public sphere.

Today, in contrast, freedom usually means an individual's ability to pursue a happiness that he or she enjoys only in private. This reality is exactly what Tocqueville feared. Tocqueville identified individualism as a major factor in the changing culture of the nineteenth century. He defined it as a "calm and considered feeling which disposes each citizen to isolate himself from the mass of his fellows and withdraw into the circle of family and friends; with this little society formed to his taste, he gladly leaves the greater society to look after itself."[4] Tocqueville was apprehensive about the future of democracy should each individual choose to stay "shut up in the solitude of his own heart."

Perhaps the most crucial change in American life has been that we have moved away from the local life of the nineteenth century, in which economic and social relationships were visible and, however imperfectly morally interpreted, viewed as parts of the larger common life. We now live in a society vastly more interrelated and integrated economically, technically, and functionally. Yet this society can only rarely understand how the self relates to this interconnected web of relations. Just as our individual identities are increasingly fragmented, so are our larger identities as communities, as a society, and as a nation.

Philosophically, our nation was born from the ideal that there exists a connection between the success of government and the happiness that

---

2. Bellah et al., *Habits of the Heart*, 285.

3. Alexis de Tocqueville, *Democracy in America*, trans. Harvey C. Mansfield and Delba Winthrop (Chicago: University of Chicago Press, 2002), vii.

4. Tocqueville, *Democracy in America*, 37.

individual citizens are able to feel. Let us not forget that happiness, according to Thomas Jefferson, is a derivative of participation in the government of affairs. The relationship between a government capable of serving the public good and citizens with a well-developed sense of personal and social responsibility is stressed in the writing by our founding fathers.

Despite years of American history lessons, I have yet to meet a student who is not surprised by this fact. While students seem to accept the idea that their lives are influenced by the collective force and feeling of culture at large, they do not seem to value the fact that their personal actions have enormous ramifications for the lives of others. I don't blame them for this profound misunderstanding of the value of participation. They come by it honestly. It has taken years to break down the organic nature of nurturance in communities. It didn't happen overnight. But the reality is that my students have trouble imagining a society in which individuals willingly work to make things better for the collective good without the motivation of compensation or reward for the individual. I can't blame them; many of these students have been taught that doing community service work is a means of getting extra credit in school or looking good on college applications.

It is a noble initiative to encourage community service work and social action. I believe in the value of engaging in service, as it encourages learning and development. Importantly, it also expands the small bubbles most of us tend to reside in by exposing us to different populations with different concerns, needs, and values. Despite these advantages, there is one clear disadvantage of our contemporary practice of tying awards and accolades to service: it reinforces the idea of separation and inequity between groups of people. And, while there is no doubt we live in a world plagued by inequalities, this system of rewarding individuals for doing what should be a natural condition of living in a connected community undermines the very values of a democratic union.

We see the philosophy of individualism working against our democratic values everywhere. It influences public policy and cultural attitudes in profound and impactful ways. Why fix our public schools? Can't those kids audition for *American Idol*? How about they win a basketball scholarship? Or (worse yet), can't they make some good choices and study hard?! This brand of individualism run amok ignores the values of social responsibility built into the American tradition of building a just and compassionate society.

This is not to say that individualism is not a positive value as well. It offers us personally unique experiences and merit-based ideals. Philosophically, it encourages ideas of free will and celebrates the differences between us in rich and meaningful ways. We really see the benefits of individualism when people who share a particular connection come together to promote new ideas or understanding. I think most of us will agree we are better off as a society due to the civil rights movement, the environmental movement, and the achievements of the LBGTQ community in recent years. But is it possible that this emphasis on individualism could be out of balance?

Helping students to begin to understand how the value of individualism has impacted their own lives is tricky. From the moment of birth, young people have soaked in a culture that celebrates the self with unbridled zeal. It is literally the life they know—an alternative version of the world feels almost Orwellian in nature. One of my favorite examples of the way individualism undermines other important values is taken from the chapter entitled "Love and Marriage" in *Habits*: "While they [respondents] wanted to maintain enduring relationships, they resisted the notion that such relationships might involve obligations that went beyond the wishes of the partners. Instead, they insisted on the 'obligation' to communicate one's wishes and feelings honestly and to attempt to deal with problems in the relationship."[5] My students blush when I read that passage aloud. It is as if they viscerally feel themselves embodied in that statement. Marriage, I offer as an alternative version, is a bit like canoeing. What happens if two people try to paddle off the same side of a canoe? It typically takes a minute before someone starts to laugh and says, "You just go around in circles." Exactly! Relationships require commitment, support, and understanding that both people have responsibilities to get to the end goal.

And, so it goes—example after example of how a different set of values might produce a different kind of community. The academic literature is chock full of these examples, but invariably, they feel flat in description. It is when we relate them to the personal that students are able to conceptualize the truth of evidence-based research. We enliven information when we teach students to "live" the information rather than simply critically evaluate it.

---

5. Bellah et al., *Habits of the Heart*, 109.

The Fashionable Nun

Individualism, unsurprisingly, also holds prime status in the field of contemporary education. But the notion that learning is a personal activity pursued by individual effort is a fallacy. The first, most basic, tenet of education is collaboration. Learning to "share" is the foundation of early learning programs. Learning is an inherently social process. And so is teaching.

One of my favorite stories about my first teaching mentor, Dorothy Kostuch, literally happened within the first moments our meeting. I had applied for an entry-level lecturing position at CCS at the suggestion of a friend. To say I was nervous about the interview is a major understatement. While my resume looked professional enough, recent years had been mostly consumed with diapers, nursery school runs, and short teaching stints at the local community house. In addition to spending a fortune on a brand-new "professional" outfit, I actually reread a few sociology classics in preparation for the interview.

My concerns that I might be quizzed on Durkheim's founding principles of sociology were immediately tossed out the window upon meeting Dr. Dorothy. (She was always known to her students as Dr. D. or Dr. Dorothy.) As I entered her office, Dorothy greeted me in her usual style—not with the obligatory, stiff, and ever-so-professional handshake, but rather with a warm embrace. She then immediately handed me the text to be used in the freshman humanities seminar and said, "Molly, I noticed you live out near Somerset Mall. I happened to leave my glasses there last week. Might you consider driving me out to pick them up? We can chat about your class on the way!"

Dorothy was something of a fascinating contradiction in terms. An ex–cloistered nun, she had, nonetheless, earned a reputation at CCS as something of a clotheshorse. Her approach to fashion was impeccable; her demeanor refined. While her Catholic faith—and its attendant emphasis on embracing the human condition—was something she put into practice in every facet of her life, there was no denying that she was a steel magnolia. Diminutive—5'1" at best—Dorothy's physical stature belied her psychological presence; she was a walking dynamo. As a former New Yorker (following her tenure as a nun, she had earned her doctorate in art history at Columbia), Dorothy had never learned to drive. While on our surprising ride to reclaim her glasses (and possibly buy some new shoes!), Dorothy made good use of our time. We discussed our favorite books, her assessment of CCS students, and the general climate at the school. She clearly outlined her expectations for adjunct faculty and challenged me to share my perspectives on teaching.

If I had to use one word to describe Dorothy, it would be passionate. Dorothy's specialty was Spanish art; she was fluent in Spanish and had studied the keystones of the Barcelona Cathedral, which were the topic of her doctoral dissertation. Her face lit up when she recounted being suspended in a small basket over 150 feet above the cathedral's floor while studying the stained glass windows. Her approach to teaching often involved hands-on work for her students. In her class Art and Culture in the Ages of Faith, when they studied Zen Buddhism and the art that accompanied it, students also participated in the Japanese tea ceremony. My future meetings with Dr. Dorothy often included being invited to sit down in one of the two armchairs opposite her desk and being presented with a cup of tea.

Community involvement was a core value for Dorothy, a fact that endeared her to me, as I share that value. Her involvement with the ultimately futile attempt to save Detroit's historical Catholic churches had resulted in a class, Art Historical Documentation, in which students researched the architecture of abandoned inner-city churches, producing both research papers and detailed drawings. Dorothy had fought to obtain permission from the Archdiocese of Detroit to enter those churches, and, typically, she had won that fight, just as she won most of her personal battles with her feisty spirit and get it done attitude.

Dorothy's office exactly reflected her personality. While the rest of the interior of the Kresge-Ford building was painted stark white, she had obtained permission to have the cinder-block walls of her office painted a warm, glowing pink. As many books as possible had been crammed into the small space, and I was impressed by their diversity. Of course, the obligatory art books were present. In addition, the Holy Bible and other books with spiritual themes of many religious orientations were placed near those whose topics were concerned with leadership and higher-education administration. It was an appropriate juxtaposition. One, in particular, interested me. Entitled *Servant Leadership*,[6] its premise was that college administrators should apply a set of practices that enrich the lives of

---

6. Robert K. Greenleaf, *Servant Leadership: A Journey into the Nature of Legitimate Power and Greatness* (Mahwah, NJ: Paulist Press, 1983).

individuals, build better educational organizations, and ultimately work to create a more just and caring world. In other words, leaders should serve those whom they lead. Dorothy believed that the element of humanity had been removed from colleges and universities and that, tragically, schools were now run by bureaucratic, corporate types who had long lost any memory of what education and administration should be.

But perhaps that which most impressed me in Dorothy's office was a small photograph of herself, impeccably dressed as always, whose caption read: "Teaching is a Work of Heart." Dorothy lived this maxim to the fullest. From the first moment we met, we connected at the level of the heart. We met as the result of a recommendation of a mutual friend. Dorothy had reviewed my resume, spoken to my former employer, and, ultimately, upon our meeting recognized that my mannerisms were socially appropriate. Dorothy trusted me. It was not blind or lazy trust, it was simultaneously both intuitive and practical.

Dr. Dorothy, with her attendant trust, taught me to see myself as competent. She influenced my craft of teaching by sharing her philosophy with me. She did this not by browbeating me into submission but by engaging me in friendship and pushing me to see myself as her equal and her colleague. I have always believed that there is a meaningful connection between philosophy and action. It is not simply a metaphorical relationship, but a practical one that impacts how we engage in activity as a result of the prevailing philosophy of those around us. As Henry Miller wrote, "Any genuine philosophy leads to action and from action back again to wonder, to the enduring fact of mystery."[7] The atmosphere that Dr. Dorothy generated in the liberal arts department that she chaired inspired competency, confidence, and creativity among my peers and within myself. By offering my colleagues and me nurturance, she encouraged the continuation of a morally driven ethic—a virtuous teaching practice. Her own example reinforced and validated my own private aspirations.

Sadly, Dr. Dorothy passed away before the creation of my course. Diagnosed with ovarian cancer, she suffered bravely and died quickly. Given the incredible pressures on teachers to follow the rubric, abide by standards, and teach online, my own observation is that teachers like Dorothy are increasingly rare gems. Dorothy was a catalyst to help me realize the learning environment that I had envisioned as a result of Charlie's healing.

---

7. Henry Miller, *The Wisdom of the Heart* (New York: New Directions, 1960), 93.

She is also one of the many angels in my museum. I am grateful to have "caught the teaching bug" from a woman who so gracefully embodied the social ecology ideals advanced by Bellah and his coauthors.

Student Paper:
Kiara—Becoming a Social Justice Superhero

My parents were children when they had me. A teenager himself, my dad became a father at the age of seventeen. An abusive, drug-dealing gangster from Ohio, the trauma inflicted on me by my dad started in utero when he threatened my mom's life by wielding a gun in her face. He never graduated high school. I suppose he came by his behavior naturally, as his mother was also a drug-dealing, high school dropout and abusive parent. My mother wasn't much better. Throughout my childhood, my mother abused me relentlessly. The only bright spot being my maternal grandmother, who was only very occasionally allowed to see me.

I learned early on that someone I loved could hurt me. It is a lesson I have learned repeatedly throughout my life. Every single act of abuse impacted my feelings about the world around me. As a young child, I imagined myself as a superhero and looked to the imaginary world of comic books and gaming for an alternative vision of what could be. As Superman proclaims in *Action Comics* #775, "Dreams save us. Dreams lift us up and transform us. And on my soul I swear: until the day when my dream of a world where dignity, honor, and justice becomes the reality we all share, I'll never stop fighting. Ever."[8]

Years of abuse have left me feeling detached. Recently, someone compared me to an emotionless robot. Ironically, it was meant as a compliment, as I do have a reputation for getting things done, but it struck me as poignant nonetheless. I am the person that everyone turns to for assistance, yet whom few know anything about. I prefer it that way, because the thought of being hurt by others again as a result is a risk I am not willing to take. I no longer fear physical pain, only emotional. For better or worse, the isolation I nurture allows me a sense of freedom. It allows me to be brave in the face of injustice.

---

8. Joe Kelly, *Superman: What's So Funny About Truth, Justice, and the American Way?* Action Comics Volume 1 #775 (New York: DC Comics, 2001).

Dear Kiara—

Sigh. It is late and I am tired. I have been reading papers on and
off all week. Somehow, probably because you emailed yours to
me, it slipped through the crack. As I checked my list of notes
written, I thought, "Kiara, where is sweet Kiara?"

I enjoy writing notes to students. I try to find inspiring
quotes relating to student stories or offer evidence from the
sociological literature that takes an argument out one step further.
With you, I am not sure where to begin. Words feel trite. What I
want to do is come find you, wrap you in my arms, and tell you I
am sorry. I am sorry that you were dealt such a devastating hand
of cards. I am sorry that you have suffered. I see you, Kiara. You
are beautiful, wise, and good.

You call yourself a pessimist. However, anyone who has
survived the trauma you recount and continued to persevere is
hardly a pessimist. Hate to break the news, but you are one hell
of an optimist! You may have gotten there in a roundabout way,
but as Anne Frank wrote, "I haven't abandoned all my ideals, they
seem so absurd and impractical. Yet I cling to them because I
still believe, in spite of everything, that people are truly good at
heart."[9]

I want to share a story with you. The year I turned twelve,
my mom dropped me off at a nursing home. I was in the market
for some new friends, and I suppose she thought Brae Burn
Nursing Home was as good a place as any other to meet some.
She was right. I met a woman named Pauline Johnson there. She
became my very good friend. She had huge boobs. It's funny to
think that that is my most distinct memory of her. I suppose it is
because her best friend in the nursing home had no boobs. She
had lost them to cancer. Before meeting Esther, I didn't know that
could happen.

We played Kings in the Corner together. It's a pretty good
card game. It requires four players. As luck would have it, I
showed up just after the death of one of the gang. Thus, the

---

9. Anne Frank, *The Diary of a Young Girl Anne: The Definitive Edition*, ed. Otto H.
Frank and Mirjam Pressler, trans. Susan Massoty (New York: Anchor Books, 1990), 333.

empty chair. The "girls" were patient with me, as I didn't have too much experience with cards. Lots of days the group felt sad—they talked about long-gone husbands, absent children, loneliness, and, of course, the universal connector: bad food. But some days, they reminded me more of my giddy middle school friends than old ladies. They cracked me up! Oh, so many funny stories—chasing children and puppies, times when cars broke down and toilets overflowed. We had fun.

In the spring of my sophomore year, I received a letter from the local Community House telling me I had been selected to win a service award. I distinctly remember feeling confused by the letter. I had never done any service work. Perhaps they had the wrong girl in mind. During the ceremony, I discovered that an administrator at the nursing home had nominated me for the honor. Looking back now, it is one of those moments that rings out with "what's wrong with this picture" meaning. Certainly, the administrator was well intentioned when she nominated me for the award. However, getting a prize for visiting the women I considered my friends devalued our relationship rather than lifting it up.

For some reason, I felt compelled to share that story with you. I don't know if it will resonate—but somehow, I think you might want to live in a world where everyone is good for the sake of being good, not because they want a reward. Can you even imagine? Talk about a cultural "superpower" make over! Being good, as you also suggest in your paper, is a simple way to transform the world. I also believe that by being good for the sake of being good, we open our hearts and enable ourselves to truly connect with other people, as I did with Pauline and my other friends at the nursing home. I think the more you act to help others, the more you will find the protective walls around your own heart slowly breaking down, and you will be able to let people in. Goodness has a way of multiplying and spreading in every direction, including back to yourself.

Love,

Molly

Fourth Week

How Do We Know Ourselves?

Your own Self-Realization is the greatest service you can render the world.

—Ramana Maharshi

The Age of the Selfie Stick

Coming home from a night out with friends, you snap a selfie and upload it to social media. In the morning, you are appalled by how tired you look in the picture, but there is something in your smile that conveys a true joy you haven't seen on your face in a while. It's easy to dismiss our culture's obsession with the self as superficial, but perhaps when we take a selfie, we are actually revealing a desire to know the true power of our singular self.

But who is that singular self, and how do we know its power? How do we differentiate the self from the social structures in which it is embedded?

Where I End and You Begin

Neurology has confirmed that the individual human brain is actually hardwired to influence other people within our social circle. In fact, there is a body of scientific evidence that personal thoughts have an infectious nature.[1] Karl Mannheim, a social philosopher and the father of the sociology of knowledge, wrote about his sense of this phenomenon in his famous book *Ideology and Utopia*.[2] It was his belief that the social emergence of collective thoughts is a reproduction of feelings, understandings, and perceptions of individuals living together in society. According to the sociology of knowledge, it is incorrect to assume that single individuals think new thoughts. Rather, we should understand that individuals participate in thinking further what other individuals have thought before.

We find meaning by living together and sharing a common culture. Culture becomes the backdrop to our lives. Interacting together in a shared milieu helps individual people to internalize ideas about expected and appropriate behavior. We internalize the social structure and come to see the status quo as a natural way of being. The way we interact and relate to each other feels right because it feels familiar. In other words, we believe things are as they are because they must be, and that we are who we are because we must be. While we may question our own thinking, we rarely question the legitimacy of the way we live together. This limits our ability to understand the complete picture of what conditions the ideas we have about our own identities and social structures.

One of my first jobs after college was as a fieldwork coordinator on a large research project at the University of Pittsburgh. My job was to interview social service administrators in three rural counties to better understand how services reached constituents. The lead researcher was working with an early (1988) version of a quantitative network analysis computer program that could map the communication patterns between administrators. In theory, understanding the map of the network would help administrators to better utilize the systems of service. I spent two years driving around western Pennsylvania talking to people. I interviewed judges, librarians, social workers, nursery school teachers, and jail wardens. I ate at little diners in small, rural communities and drank coffee with the locals. I met amazing people and heard unbelievable stories. Stories of strength, tragedy, hope, and despair. Flying over the hills in my little

---

1. Nicholas A. Christakis and James H. Fowler, *Connected: The Surprising Power of Our Social Networks and How They Shape Our Lives—How Your Friends' Friends' Friends Affect Everything You Feel, Think, and Do* (New York: Little, Brown, 2011).

2. Karl Mannheim, *Ideology and Utopia: An Introduction to the Sociology of Knowledge* (Eastford, CT: Martino Fine Books, 2015).

GT hatchback Colt, I discovered worlds within worlds that I never knew existed.

The end result of the data collection resulted in web-like images of the various connections in the social service community. They looked like constellation drawings and confused most everyone upon first glance. When I was explaining the graphs during a meeting, the head of the juvenile probation office interrupted me and asked seriously, "What's a nice girl like you doing with that crazy spider lady from the University?" Here's the funny thing: at the time, I was equally confused by much of what we found. It is only now, many years later, that I can see how meeting those administrators and asking those questions trained me to look for the big picture made up by the small data points.

We discovered some nice surprises embedded in the social networks in western Pennsylvania, specifically a small preschool program, Helping Hands, that seemed to be linked to every power player in the county. Run out of a church basement by a beloved community elder, this little program seemed to be a source of support for everyone in the community. I distinctly remember the preschool director's surprise at noticing the very central and large dot her tiny school had received on the web of local connections. In our final wrap-up presentation, she received lots of kudos as individuals suddenly realized the important impact her work had on the whole of the system.

During graduate school, my work in western Pennsylvania was echoed many times over, perhaps most brilliantly in the book *Power and Powerlessness: Quiescence and Rebellion in an Appalachian Valley* by John Gaventa.[3] In this award-winning book, Gaventa reveals that the real source of power in an industrial society is the ability to establish control for generating consensus: "The total impact of a power relationship is more than the sum of its parts. Power serves to create power. Powerlessness serves to re-enforce powerlessness. Power relationships, once established, are self-sustaining."[4] Individuals believe in the legitimacy of the social structure. Societal norms legitimize the dominant values and concerns of society. The powerless embody their own status as personal to them; they

---

3. John Gaventa, *Power and Powerlessness: Quiescence and Rebellion in an Appalachian Valley* (Urbana: University of Illinois Press, 1982).

4. Gaventa, *Power and Powerlessness*, 256.

often stay isolated from each other and unaware that others feel the same way. As a result, power works not only to maintain itself but to establish a general consensus view that things are the way they are because it is in the best interest of the whole of society. We collectively accept our status and reinforce it through interaction, thoughts, and beliefs in the legitimacy of our way of life.

In simple terms, every bully needs a victim, every nurse a patient, every teacher a student, and so on. In essence, the world that our reason tries to sustain is the world that is created by the descriptions around us. Reasonable people find ways to accept and defend the patterns that sustain their status—even if they perceive their status to be wrongly judged or unfairly given. We confirm over and over again the righteousness of the plot by picking up the thread of all that has been thought before.

How do we know ourselves? We know ourselves by knowing others.

"A Dangerous Move Away from Academic Standards!"

By 2008, CCS, like many other colleges and universities, experienced an exponential growth in a new tier of management influences. Due to increasing emphasis on "outcome-oriented" education models and accreditation demands, there was a noticeable increase in bureaucratic control being exerted over the teaching process at CCS. To be honest, some of this was needed. My own teaching evolved in a positive direction when I was pushed to reorganize my syllabus to include outcome-oriented learning expectations. That said, the exaggerated push to emphasize specific goals over process slowly started to chip away at any sense of creative freedom in the classroom.

I remember reading an article a few years ago comparing the absurdity of a bureaucrat with no classroom experience being in charge of managing teachers to a restaurant manager with no taste buds designing a menu. Someone with no sense of taste will evaluate what the menu looks like, how many minutes the salad takes to get to the table, and how many words the waiter uses when describing the specials. Similarly, the hand-wringing over grading rubrics, streamlined assignment postings, and attendance policies maintains evaluation as the primary goal of teaching from a management perspective. Additionally, and ironically, as these factors come into play, you need more and more managers to gather information, analyze data, and file accreditation reports. In this model, education becomes a hyperbureaucracy: Managers managing managers who manage administrators, and so on. Where do teachers fit into this equation? And, more importantly, what impact does this ultimately have on student experience?

Like most shifts, the first symptoms of this college-wide change were subtle. Our new liberal arts chair insisted that every syllabus in the department use a template to insure uniformity. The department became much more hierarchical in nature. No more off-campus lunch meetings. Our time together needed to be recorded with the minutes posted and made available to all online later. The plagiarism contract became the Holy Grail of every faculty meeting (how many times could we rewrite the darn thing?). We started using the technological learning management system Blackboard. As a result, a large number of our responsibilities were now tied to maintaining and updating our courses online. Words like "assign," "comprehend," "analyze," and "evaluate" became the drumbeat of every conversation within the department. And, finally, over the course of a couple semesters, a dozen or so long-time adjunct faculty members found that their courses were simply no longer listed as course offerings.

The impact of these changes left many of my colleagues feeling a new fragility about our roles at the college. Teaching began to feel more mechanistic in nature—task oriented and, often, burdensome. There were fewer opportunities to become meaningfully involved on campus. Management set policy. No longer were adjunct faculty members invited to the table. Given the fact that the liberal arts department employed upward of 85 percent adjuncts, that essentially silenced the majority of stakeholders. Any fluidity of process was lost in the quest to maintain the managerial hierarchy. While policy certainly trickled down, ideas rarely trickled up. The ability of individual instructors to have input became greatly reduced.

It was amid this new climate that the staff began trying to address the problem of student stress and disengagement. Though it did not exactly fit into the college's increasingly outcome-oriented philosophy, I confidently proposed a course integrating meditation called "Consciousness, Creativity, and Identity" to be taught as an elective in the liberal arts department.

It has been said that creating new curriculum initiatives is akin to moving a graveyard down the street. All the old theorists must be dug up in order to justify any shift in perspective. One of my favorite fictional scenes in literature remains Richard Russo's hilarious telling of the roundtable discussion at an English departmental meeting in the novel *Straight Man*.[5] The meeting ends with a particularly aggressive poet smacking the department chair in the face with a spiral notebook.

When I first proposed integrating meditation into the core curriculum of an academic course, the chair of my department pounded her fists on the table in anger. She literally screamed, "This will never happen during my tenure at this school! A course like this is a dangerous move away from academic standards!" In her mind, my course represented a radical departure from traditional liberal arts expectations. Fortunately, for my students and me, her tenure in the chair seat was short. And, when a more open-minded critical theorist stepped into her office, a call to me was at the top of his agenda. The course initially ran as a one-semester experimental offering. It took four semesters of overenrollment, a student-led campaign, and a meeting with the full faculty assembly to eventually confirm an established course number. To say this was an unusually lengthy and demanding approval process is an understatement. The existence of this course threatened many of my colleagues' notions of academia and their place in it.

Perhaps the most interesting aspect of the entire process of getting my class on the books was learning to speak the institutional language—in other words, figuring out what everyone wanted to hear and producing some evidence that my class could meet the extraordinarily varied needs of an institution. For example, the counseling department at CCS really liked the research on meditation as related to stress reduction, the film department really liked the research on meditation as related to enhanced creativity, and the administration liked the research on meditation as linked to retention rates. Many in my own department expressed concern that my proposed class would not be rigorous enough. I had to produce a long reading list, a research paper assignment, and detailed learning outcomes and assure my chair that the meditation component was simply an experiential tool. Piecing together the fragmented expectations of my varied stakeholders became a full-time preoccupation. It also represented a pretty interesting view of the contemporary educational landscape. And "fragmented" is an apt word to describe it.

There has been much written on the impact of specialization in academia. Certainly, it is well documented that our economy requires

---

5. Richard Russo, *Straight Man* (New York: Vintage, 1998), 20.

increased specialization and well-developed technical skills. That said, when education becomes an instrument for individual careerism, it no longer inspires students in broad, sweeping terms. Importantly, specialization also ignores the connections between all the abstract pieces of information that make up the whole. While it may be impossible to know everything, it is imperative that different disciplines work together to grow our understanding of each other and the world around us. Perhaps our greatest challenge today is to figure out how the whole of humanity becomes greater than the sum of its individual parts.

Thinking influences both the personal and the collective. This is why including a meditation practice in the classroom solves for the issues of limitation in education. Spending time in silence allows one to transcend the daily input of distractions, noise, and stress. The repeated action of sitting in silence incrementally builds more and more purity of thought—less stress and more openness. This openness leads to an ability to connect information from disparate sources and perceive how it fits together. It also translates to a healthier environment for all of us collectively. A truly integrative educational model is one that does not merely stack discipline on top of discipline, but one that literally enlivens the learning process by teaching students to touch their most transcendent natures, reminding them of who they really are and how much they really know.

Student Paper: Tyler—Up and Out of the Rabbit Hole

There was a long portion of my life that I spent hating myself so badly. The thought of suicide entered my head almost daily. More recently, I have come to realize that I may be my own worst enemy. My life is too often spent wrestling with the existential conditions of my own being.

I don't remember feeling this way as a young child. In fact, my extended family love to regale me with tales of my witty, outgoing, childish, younger self. This pattern of morose longing may have been unwittingly set in motion during my sixth birthday party.

I was born to a relatively affluent family. My father ran a small business that he inherited from his father. This business generated a fair amount of wealth and respect in our suburban community. For my sixth birthday party, my dad organized a party. Even at six, I knew this party had as much to do with "setting me up" to be successful in kindergarten as it did with celebrating my birth. The party was a grand event held in a ballroom. My parents invited all the children that were to be in my class the following fall. There were presents, music, and a most spectacular surprise: a magician! I was totally enthralled by him, envious of how he could amuse and amaze his audience. He seemed to be able to spread joy effortlessly.

The highlight of the afternoon occurred when he handed me a spoon to bend. It seemed that I, too, possessed an innate talent to surprise and mesmerize my peers. The spoon unexplainably bent as I rubbed it gently between my fingers. I could feel myself becoming addicted to the feeling of being powerful, the master of the moment. The excitement in the room was palpable.

What followed the spoon trick surpassed my wildest expectations: the magician pulled a mother-lovin' rabbit out of his hat. He immediately handed it to me—the birthday boy! I pressed that beautiful, white rabbit to my face, clinging to it in selfish adoration. I was immediately surrounded by my soon-to-be classmates eagerly reaching over for a pat. I had never felt more special, more joyous, or more alive. Yet, it was in that exact moment that I learned that every experience contains hidden dimensions. For as I slowly turned within the circle of my friends, my face furiously turned red, blotchy, and swollen. It appeared that I was horribly allergic to rabbit fur.

A gallon of Benadryl later, my friends gone from the venue, my parents calmed, I found my magician sitting at the bar. Midway through a tall scotch—or maybe bourbon—my hero presented as the loneliest, saddest man on the planet. My own humiliation, shame, and sorrow paled in comparison to the depth of his dejected spirit. It occurred to me as I sat with my former hero that in every moment a multitude of emotions commingle. The moment of shame was not mine alone; it belonged to the magician too. Our interaction was a shared experience. I shyly apologized to him for losing his spoon. He chuckled, rifled through his jacket, and handed me another. While it may sound dramatic, life never felt the same again. The jarring recognition that interactions with others might reflect my inner emotions thrust such hopeless self-consciousness into my psyche that I felt paralyzed to interact with anyone without the burden of this knowing. My subjective sensitivity had yet to be met with my objective understanding.

Dear Tyler—

Transformation can come from nearly endless sources. The story of the magician is a wonderfully charged example of a moment of awakening. The spontaneity of the events unfolded in such a twisted way that your own pain was reflected back to you with such profound symbolism. In the end, the magic show was literally just that—magic—infused with meaning and resonance. This moment of awareness offered you the first glimpse of your connection to others. Your ability to see yourself reflected in the eyes of your sorrowful magician surprised you in unexpected ways. The easy mistake you made was assuming that you were the source of all his pain.

Shame is the internalized fear that others think poorly of you. Guilt, shame's stepsister in crime, is the internal fear of wrongdoing. Sometimes guilt and shame stem from some twisted narrative we have believed for too long. My mother often reminds me, "Guilt is just anger turned inward." Your six-year-old self must have felt so mad about being allergic to that sweet, soft bunny rabbit. Your allergies had ruined an otherwise perfect moment of stardom!

The bigger disappointments you faced during your teenage years all mirror this sensation of being responsible for the feelings of everyone around you. I understand how this might lead you to pull back from interacting with others. But, there you have it: a push/pull dynamic that leaves you stuck evaluating the confusion you feel and too often paralyzed by indecisive angst to enter the web of relationships you see as extensions of yourself.

Another student shared the following story in her paper: While she was innocently sitting at the kitchen table eating a bowl of soup, her dad had a massive temper tantrum of rage at her mother and siblings that finished with him turning to her and screaming, "And, you, young lady, will begin to eat meat again!" She wrote: "It was so over-the-top ridiculous that I finally realized his behavior wasn't personal to me—it was his issues just spilling out all over the place." This story is a classic, and confirms the following: people behave out of how *they* feel; their behavior is not personal to you, it is personal only to them.

In the end, Tyler, all problems are essentially relationship problems; dividing them into various categories is an error. The solution starts in caring for others. As my own mentor taught me, connectedness starts when one individual consciously chooses to extend caring presence to other. This is done by offering pure recognition, absent of evaluation—by listening. The art of listening—to yourself, to others, to nature, to culture—is the only way up and out of the rabbit hole. Many people are unable to do this, as they wish to remain aloof in righteousness and evaluation. Sometimes, this is just because they are fearful of what they might see. But the way to solve a problem is by getting "in it," not sitting aloof and alone, but studying, talking, or writing about it.

There is a certain beauty in your story of the magician. To me, it offers further evidence that the world cannot be explained. To understand the infinite, eternal reality is not actually even the goal of individualized beings. Rather, the "trick" is to accept the mystery and slowly gain *realization* through conscious, subjective experience. If we are lucky, we all run into the proverbial magician from time to time: a moment of grace that reveals the indescribable to us. Looking back from the vantage of young adulthood, can't you sympathize with that young boy just trying to do his best in a confusing web of expectations?

I sent you some additional references in a second attachment. Nice job.

Love,

Molly

Fifth Week

How Does the World around Us Inform Our Sense of Self?

Thanks for a wonderful class, Molly! Before class, I had started to figure some of this stuff out. But, taking this class, and being here with you, validated everything I had begun to understand. It's one thing to suspect you're not crazy but to have someone that doesn't owe you anything confirm it is really healing!

Much love, Rebecca

Swimming through the Blue Pool

Years ago, when my kids were little, they loved a movie called *Big Fat Liar*. Typical of the kid movie genre, the movie showcased the kids outsmarting the adults in a myriad of ways. In one clever scene, the young heroes pour blue dye in a backyard swimming pool. The unsuspecting adult villain, Marty, jumps in for a swim, only to emerge as a Smurf-like character drenched in blue. What makes the scene particularly funny—at least to my children—is the fact that Marty doesn't initially recognize that the joke is on him. The scene is completed with a dancing blueberry Marty making his way back into his home, completely unaware of his ridiculous appearance.

The Sociological Imagination

I use this simple analogy to introduce students to C. Wright Mills's classic concept known as the "sociological imagination." A sociological imagination enables individuals to cope with the social world by helping them to step outside their own personal, self-focused view of the world. By thinking in more objective terms, people are encouraged to perceive how certain events and social structures influence individual behavior, attitudes, and culture.

Think of a fish swimming in the ocean. The fish is surrounded by water, but the water is so familiar and normalized, we might assume that the fish would struggle to describe the qualities of the water. Similarly, we all live in the social milieu, but because we are so intimately familiar with it, we struggle to see our situations objectively. Metaphorically, we don't realize we get soaked in the blue dye of the cultural swimming pool! In his 1959 book, *The Sociological Imagination*, Mills referenced the fast-moving changes of society and his concern that "the very shaping of history now outpaces the ability of men to orient themselves in accordance with their cherished values."[1] My students always react to this line with surprise—noting the ironic combination of such astute observations about the future commingling with such backward gendered language. It offers a great opportunity to explore how even the best theorists are stuck in a time warp of historical proportions. That fact shouldn't distract us from the validity of the overarching arguments of the work; it should simply remind us of the contextual environment that influences even the most objective of knowledge.

Importantly, in his book, Mills outlines the ways in which values are connected to feelings of well-being. According to Mills, when people cherish some set of values and feel no threat to those values, they experience a feeling of well-being. However, if they feel a threat to those values, they will experience a personal crisis. If all of their values are threatened, individuals will panic. But, what if, Mills proposes, people are unaware of any of their cherished values? If they have no threats, they likely live with some indifference or, perhaps, apathy. But, what if individuals are simultaneously unaware of their values but very aware of threats? Would they not experience anxiety, proposes Mills? Aha! says the blind man. With this short assessment of cultural "what if's," Mills succinctly takes the pulse of an entire generation.

Breaking down this idea is pretty simple. Everyone can play with a mental picture of themselves eating delicious, organic food with their

---

1. C. Wright Mills, *The Sociological Imagination* (London: Oxford University Press, 1959), 4.

family and friends. Stretching the image out might include birds singing, music playing, and children laughing. From every angle, the image soothes the senses: it *feels* peaceful, safe, and, importantly, devoid of threats. The idyllic scenario encompasses both the obvious values of family, friends, and nurturance and the more abstract values of clean air, safe food sources, and community membership. In contrast, it's pretty easy to imagine the kind of panic that an air-raid siren followed by a dive bomber hurtling through the eastern sky would inspire.

In 1977, when I was eleven years old, I had my own paper route and a huge amount of freedom. The newspaper, *The Eccentric*, was dropped at my house every Tuesday and Thursday morning. I would arrive home from school, unbundle and roll the papers, and put them in my little red wagon. My route only covered a few blocks, but it took an hour or two to complete the task. In the winter, I would finish up at dusk. I quit the job before the end of the school year.

In the early spring of 1977, a young boy from my community was kidnapped and murdered. Timmy King was the fourth child to be abducted and later killed in Oakland County. The case remains unsolved. Timothy King was my same age—would have graduated with me from high school if he had lived. The fear and vulnerability that resulted from the murder settled on our neighborhood like a heavy cloak of darkness. I can't remember now if the loss of my paper route was due to my own fear or my mother's protectionist reactivity. Either way, the carefree atmosphere that had enveloped my early childhood evaporated immediately in the face of such close-up horror.

The ability to point to this one event in my own life allows me to create a narrative that justifies the changes that happened in the cultural atmosphere throughout my childhood. Timmy King exists in my mind as a page turn. There was a before and an after. The fear I felt and the protectionist parenting that followed made sense to me. The world was scary because kidnappers could come and snatch me. But, if I stayed close to home, didn't talk to strangers, and paid attention, I could keep myself safe. In an ironic way, this event introduced both fear and safety to me: terrible things happen, but can potentially be avoided too. My own preciousness was confirmed by the reaction of my parents and my community to the loss of Timmy. There was a knowable, close-up quality to the events of the winter of 1977 in Birmingham, Michigan.

Now, take a typical freshman college student—born in 2000, on the eve of the 9/11 terrorist attacks, this is a child who entered the world on the cusp of deep societal changes. Terrorism, the plague of the twenty-first century, is defined by violence that produces "widespread disproportional emotional reactions such as fear and anxiety which are likely to influence attitudes and behavior."[2] The whole goal of terrorism is to convey a message that violence can happen at any time or in any place. Threats are intended to be unpredictable. There is no way to stay safe because no space is immune to the randomness of attack. Thus, the goal is to gain social control through fear.

In the 2017–18 Healthy Minds Study, an annual web-based survey examining mental health on college campuses, the number of CCS students who scored positive on a measure of depression was nearly equal, at 23 percent, to the number who scored positive on a measure of anxiety, 24 percent. According to Val Weiss, MSW, CCS's Wellness Center director, depression and anxiety function as two sides of the same coin. According to Val, "Students know that something isn't right, but they struggle to identify just what that something is. It's as if they're always looking over their shoulder in fear of the proverbial lion. Never 'seeing' their predator makes them feel 'crazy.' They just float in this constant amorphous feeling of unmoored anxiety or sadness. It can be really tough for young people to navigate this cultural landscape." Getting young people to think about how the unique historical/cultural circumstances have impacted their own lives helps them to grow compassion for both themselves and others.

It's easy enough to list the tragedies of human history—wars, starvation, poverty, and disease—that litter our collective memory. Yet do we ever stop to truly think about how these events reverberate throughout time? How they impact our day-to-day experience of ourselves? How do we ride the "fumes" of these traumas? Taken together, Mills and Bellah offer us a unique perspective on the challenges we face. Our inability to articulate collective values, combined with undefined threats that seem to come from everywhere and nowhere at the same time, renders us filled with indefinable anxiety and discomfort. Developing a sociological imagination helps us realize that the anxiety that may plague us is a product of our historical and cultural context and not unique to our individual lives. We learn from understanding the intersection of personal biography and cultural context—using a sociological imagination implies being

---

2. Gregor Bruce, "Definition of Terrorism—Social and Political Effects," *Journal of Military and Veterans' Health* 21, no. 2 (2013): 26–30.

firmly planted in the here and now, while simultaneously understanding the trajectory of events and beliefs that helped get us here.

The Legacy of Knitting

I was in a knitting club for a brief and rather disastrous time—there is proof in a lopsided, unfinished baby's hat that sits in the cabinet (collecting dust) above my washer. My non-gender-specific cap was red and navy blue with a curled-up lip that was intended to frame the chubby face of my eagerly anticipated third baby. I knitted it over one long winter while drinking wine in various girlfriends' homes. The houses were invariably bigger and grander than mine, and I spent most of my time thinking about why these wealthy women were knitting as a hobby. It felt contrived, in a way. One of the women had a collection of eighteenth-century Native American etchings going up her stairwell. I was mesmerized by those images staring down at us while we knitted away painfully.

My grandmother was a beautiful knitter. She taught me to knit as a little girl, and it remains one of my favorite memories. We sat side by side on her black corduroy couch. My grandmother's house was filled with all kinds of cool stuff: a crystal jar full of sugared gumdrops, porcelain figurines, and, my absolute favorite, a wallpapered mahogany box made up to look like a miniature dining room. The one-room, mini-dollhouse even had a cut-out silhouette hanging on the wallpapered wall and a set of silver candlesticks on the table. I don't know why I always loved that little box, but I did. It was the kind of thing that you could only touch with two fingers. You would have to kneel on the sofa, gingerly reach up, and pet the table and chairs. It felt decadent.

Anyway, my nana taught me to knit—pearl one, knit two, and so on. Charlotte—or Lottie, as her friends called her—loved all kinds of needlework: sewing, crocheting, knitting, and so on. In fact, one of my most cherished possessions remains a large needlepoint pillow that she designed and created a few years before her death. It is beautiful and intricate—perfectly finished without a missed stitch or an unfinished edge.

Despite her versatility with a needle, there was one pattern that my grandmother repeatedly returned to throughout her life: a baby sweater with owls on it. She used a rough, thin yarn that came in white, pale blue-and-pink, and the softest yellow you have ever seen. Around the yoke of the sweater were a series of little owls with button eyes. She made the sweaters for the newborn infants of girlfriends, for unknown children in different hospitals, for her grandchildren, and, ultimately, for my children—her great-grandchildren.

When my nana and I knitted together, we always used the baby sweater yarn. While I don't remember asking for different yarn, I do remember feeling a bit frustrated by my limited choice of palette and curious about her commitment to making and remaking the same baby sweater. It was not until I was a young teenager that I gained any real insight into my nana's obsession with baby yarn. It turns out that during the too-hot summer of 1947, my grandmother had lost a postdue baby boy during a difficult delivery. His death completely devastated both of my grandparents. I don't believe either of them ever fully recovered from the loss.

Picking up needles during the winter of my knitting club immersion experience actualized an immediate sense of recognition. Sitting in those lovely living rooms, knitting my navy-and-red baby cap, I felt a strong and immediate connection to my grandmother. I would wonder to myself: What did my nana think about while she knit that owl pattern over and over again for close to sixty years? Did she think about the day her baby boy died? Or recall the years afterward when my mother would come home to find all the doors and windows open and my nana crying alone in a closet? Did she think about the lost potential? The little boy who might have saved her—all the could haves, would haves, what might have beens?

There is something about knitting. Perhaps it is the repetitive nature of it—hands distracted, the mind can wander freely. I found myself fantasizing about my own expanding family, my desires, and my own "becoming" into womanhood. Under the gaze of those soulful Native American eyes, I thought about traditions: the way we naturally and automatically tend to pick up the threads of the lives that came before. How we carry the grief of loss into each generation with our fear for the future and our superstitious commitment to age-old practices that feel comfortable in their familiarity. Sometimes, in a quiet moment, I found myself thinking about all those little owl sweaters: Did they lie folded neatly in parchment paper at the bottom of sweet-smelling cedar boxes? Or does a tiny, precious newborn in Cambodia wear one home from the hospital? How do our grief and our healing spill out into the world?

It is important every once in a while to examine the reasons we engage in certain activities. The connection between our personal life and our cultural history. What was my knitting really about? Why wasn't I skydiving or painting? Knitting somehow got tied up in my own ideas of what it meant to be a mother. While it never really became my thing, knitting that one winter did help me untangle the story of my grand-mother's grief and its impact on our family. Knitting, along with thinking about knitting, offered me a lens through which to use my sociological imagination. As C. Wright Mills writes, "The sociological imagination enables its possessor to understand the larger historical scene in terms of its meaning for the inner life and the external career of a variety of individuals. It enables him to take into account how individuals, in the welter of their daily experience, often become falsely conscious of their social positions. Within that welter, the framework of modern society is sought, and within that framework the psychologies of a variety of men and women are formulated."[3]

I didn't last too long in that knitting club. I joined a book club a few years later. We drink wine too. It's all good.

Student Paper: Kelly—Part of the "Bitch Clique"

Social media reinforces the evaluative tendency of middle school girls. There is constant commentary on outward qualities of appearance, attrac-tiveness, clothing, and makeup. No matter how hard I try, it is difficult to avoid being influenced by the harsh judgment of the online world. I'm not sure if my "real life" imitates my "Insta life" or vice versa, but the mirroring qualities of both worlds left me feeling pretty bloodied and bruised by the end of high school. As if it's not painful enough to navigate the hallways of my own school, at any given time someone in Denver can hurl a slur my way.

Growing up in my affluent, materialistic community felt like climbing an imaginary ladder every single day. Sometimes it felt like this metaphorical ladder dangled precipitously over a den of open-mouthed, salivating tigers. I'm telling you, Lulu Lemon-clad young women are flipping warriors who could likely solve the Middle East peace crisis with their sharp tongues and no-holds-barred prison mentality. It makes it hard to find happiness when there is always so much pressure to "one-up" our friends.

I grew up in a very verbally abusive family. My dad is wonderful in lots of ways, but he drinks too much and alcohol brings out his very bad

---

3. Mills, *Sociological Imagination*, 5.

temper. A lot of screaming, yelling, and crying went on in my household. So much, in fact, that it became the norm for our communication.

My dad's inclination was to be protective. One night after I got in trouble for staying too late at a friend's house, he decided I would no longer be allowed to leave the house. Over time this punishment cycle became routine. Sometimes, I didn't even know what I had done wrong. My parents' yelling lost its meaning over time. It seemed I was never allowed to hang out with my friends. I felt so trapped. At this point, the punishments felt outsized to the nature of my crimes. My bad behavior was typically linked to wanting to be with my friends more than my family, staying out late, or talking back to my mom.

Over time, however, I started disobeying my parents' every rule. I just felt so caged and misunderstood. No matter what I did, I knew I risked punishment, so why not have some fun along the way? I started running away from home. I truly felt—at age fourteen—that I didn't need my parents. I lied about pretty much everything. When my parents thought I was at work, I was at a concert. When they thought I was at cheer practice, I was in my friend's basement drinking. That's when I started to become very independent. I never asked for money. I got my own rides and bought my own stuff.

My attitude was one of hostility. My strained relationship with my parents was similar to my relationships with my friends. I didn't have too many, and the ones I did have weren't good for me. They influenced me to make some bad choices, do some dumb things, and take some real risks. The mean-girl, drama-queen, gossipy atmosphere surrounded me. Looking back, I can see that I was both a participator and a promoter of the bitch clique. I started getting attention from boys for being both curvy and on the cheer team. (Throw up in my mouth—stereotype). Rumor had it that I was a whore, a slut, fat and ugly.

One day I was walking to my class, and a girl that I never talked to came up to me along with her friends. She got in my face, threatening me about talking to her "man," and without giving me a chance to say anything, all three of them attacked me. I was confused, shocked, and scared. At that moment, all I could think about was defending myself so I fought back. From then on no one ever messed with me again and people were actually going out of their way to be nice to me. I was "cool" for fighting and protecting myself. In some ways, this was a really positive experience. I learned to defend myself, have thick skin, and not let people push me around. But, the sad consequence of these years is losing the silly, weird, shy little girl who I liked being.

The biggest lesson I will take from this semester is the idea that "everyone's behavior is a reflection of how they feel and not necessarily personal to me." I wish I'd understood that in high school. The first time you said that in class, I felt so confused. It was like being hit in the head with a two-by-four. Over the past few weeks, I've just reminded myself over and over again of all the times I've reacted in my own pain, frustration, sadness, or hurt. Knowing this helps me to view others with a little bit more compassion and openness. In high school I worried constantly about what others thought of me, what a waste of time.

Dear Kelly—

The challenges of growing up in an affluent suburb where materialistic values reign front and center are quite real. Being socially successful—popular—is a highly valued trait. Some parents are slow to punish children for drinking or other "delinquent" behaviors because they fear the kids missing out on "all the fun." Heaven forbid you stay in on a Saturday night—you might lose your spot in the pecking order. The emphasis on social success combined with the enormous pressure to know exactly what you want to "do" when you are an adult stunts young people's ability to grow an authentic identity based on true natural inclination. While it sounds like your parents understood the risks inherent to this culture, coming down hard on you due to their own fears likely confused and angered you.

There is a certain irony in the way beauty is celebrated in our culture. While we revere physical beauty on the screen, in magazines, and in theory, we are often intimidated and confused by it when faced with it in our everyday life. Sometimes people perceive beautiful people as naturally embodying the "false" or superficial values of our cultural definition of beauty. My hunch is that you ran into this conundrum a bunch of times—you probably terrified your father, intimidated your peers, produced envy in all the girls, and attracted every boy in Oakland County. Faced with all that reaction, you likely felt annoyed that no one could "SEE" you—the true you—and that probably pissed you off. And so, the cycle began . . .

For the record, I detect a strength, determination, and intelligence in you that lives far beneath the surface of your beauty. More importantly, I see you starting to tap into that awareness. Your paper shows such a lovely, forgiving spirit. Despite your hurt and regret, you do not seem angry at yourself or others. Navigating the teenage years is difficult under the best of circumstances. Sounds to me as if you have not always been treated so well or "seen" completely by the people you love the most. That hurts. But your growing awareness that other people's behavior is not personal to you will help you to form healthier relationships in the future and, I suspect, allow you to embrace who you really are.

Love,

Molly

Sixth Week

Who Is Responsible?

If we could change ourselves, the tendencies in the world would also change. As a man changes his own nature, so does the attitude of the world change towards him. . . . We need not wait to see what others do.

—Mahatma Gandhi

The Burn Unit

During my senior year of college, I interned at the University of Michigan Hospital burn unit. At the time, I was considering a career in social work and wanted to learn about how the hospital and the related systems of social support worked together. If you'll forgive the pun: talk about trial by fire!

Hospital burn units are pretty intense places. As a young twenty-one year old, I felt completely overwhelmed by the magnitude of suffering I witnessed over the course of the semester. Ultimately, the experience also led me to realize that navigating the complicated bureaucratic maze that social work entailed was not a good fit for me. For years, I thought about that internship with a sense of personal failure and even embarrassment. I had not taken to social work, and I had felt unprepared for being immersed in a world of acute pain, skin grafts, and complicated medical situations. Frankly, the entire experience intimidated and frightened me.

Fifteen years later, my parents were at a fundraiser—wearing name tags—when they were approached by a gentleman who asked them if they happened to know a woman named Molly with the same last name.

When they replied, "Yes, Molly is our daughter," he cracked a huge smile and said, "Oh, what a lovely daughter you have!" He then proceeded to tell my parents how I had sat with his father as he lay dying in the burn unit all those years ago. "She told him countless stories and jokes. Her sunny enthusiasm brought my dad so much peace and good humor during his final days." He then asked my parents to please send me his love and best wishes.

When my mother called me the following morning to share the story, a rush of emotions flooded my mind. Only then did I understand that the value of that internship was not the little I had learned about skin grafts or the way a hospital functions. The value of that time was that I had simply sat with another human at the end of his life. When I heard about the impact my caring presence had had on that man and his family, I was able to see that internship in the burn unit in a whole new light. My perception that the experience had been a failure was completely transformed by this new information. Not only did I now have a lens through which to understand my personal impact, I remembered all I had learned from interacting with so many different people in such a stressful environment.

The Connections between
Individual and Cultural Failures

Every now and again, I meet a student who utterly upends my sense of the world around me. A few years ago, one such student graced my classroom with her spirit. Tiny in stature, Sarah made up for it with the weight of her wisdom. Her hair changed colors on a week-to-week basis—bright blue, streaked purple, hot pink. She dressed like an animated character in neon colors and childlike dresses; porcelain skin and black Goth-like boots rounded out her look. From the moment I first laid my eyes on her, I was entranced.

At the end of the semester, Sarah wrote me a thank you note. In it she expressed her gratitude for being "seen" as more than just an eccentric dresser and anxiety-ridden student. She wrote: "You know, after I recovered from the mental illness I never really believed I suffered from—but that my parents and doctors insisted I had—I realized I was simply traumatized by growing up in the harshness of this world." She went on to describe the experience of being so sensitive that she could viscerally feel the playground cruelty—whether it was directed to her or not. Her connection to others was so strong, her empathy so well developed that watching others suffer in life or on the big screen rendered her hurt, scared, and confused. As she said, "I just couldn't understand why in a world of so much beauty, the commitment to hurting each other overrode the ease of kindness and compassion."

We live in a culture that frames failures as individual rather than cultural or institutional. The truth is few of us define the personal troubles we face as outgrowths of the shifting nature of culture. People typically assume that social problems such as poverty, unemployment, or even eating disorders stem from personal failings of individuals experiencing the problems versus structural issues in the larger society. Mills suggests that thinking of social problems as personal troubles ignores the public issues that contribute to the creation of the problems in the first place.

Take, for example, unemployment: if only a few people are unemployed, Mills wrote, we could understand their unemployment as being the result of personal laziness, lack of good work habits, showing up late, and so forth. If so, their unemployment would be due to their own personal failings. But when millions of people are out of work, unemployment is best understood as a public issue because, as Mills writes, "the very structure of opportunities has collapsed. Both the correct statement of the problem and the range of possible solutions require us to consider the economic and political institutions of the society, and not merely the personal situation and character of a scatter of individuals."[1]

When we attempt to understand our perceived failings strictly on the individual level, we wrongly embody those failures as personal. Despite the obvious cultural influence, our anxiety becomes indicative of our own inadequacies and mental deficiencies. In failing to see the whole picture, we shame ourselves into private isolated suffering.

In the instance of the burn unit internship, I viewed my inability to identify a potential future job in the hospital as a personal failure. There was no one practical task that appealed to me as a potential career. The intangible nature of need that my presence fulfilled in the hospital could not be validated by a job description. And, in the case of Sarah, her feelings of weakness, confusion, and anxiety were tied to her ability to

---

1. C. Wright Mills, *The Sociological Imagination* (London: Oxford University Press, 1959), 9.

"feel" the undercurrent of emotions that fueled the bad behavior around her. The outside world overwhelmed her fragile nervous system. Rather than working to correct the environment that she lived and breathed in, she was judged by her reaction to it. This is a nuanced situation and one that requires deep thoughtfulness and sensitivity to fix.

Several years ago, a group of students produced a group project that stunned me. They wrote a research paper about the causes, symptoms, and increasing rates of ADD/ADHD across the country. They stood in front of a sleekly designed poster they had made while giving their final presentation. The poster offered an image of a pretty kitchen filled with all the expected bells and whistles: on the shiny, white counter there was a brown-bag lunch, an apple . . . and a syringe. Looking at the image felt like getting punched in the face by a Ray Bradbury sci-fi story come to life. The precision and insight offered by those students during their twenty-minute presentation literally sent chills down my back.

In his controversial book, *The Myth of the A.D.D. Child*, Dr. Thomas Armstrong argues that many of the behaviors labeled as ADD and ADHD are simply a child's active response to complex social, emotional, and educational influences.[2] In his well-reasoned, evidence-based book, Armstrong argues that kids can be hyperactive for any number of reasons, including boredom, a different kind of learning style, anxiety or depression, overstimulation from television or video games, and lack of sleep. The problem is lumping all these disparate symptoms together to create a diagnosis of ADD or ADHD while ignoring the underlying issues that cause the behavior. While Armstrong acknowledges the epidemic of hyperactivity seen in today's children, he questions our race to tag kids with a psychiatric diagnosis so quickly.

If you feel your head bobbing in agreement with Armstrong's thesis, imagine how my young college students feel when they hear the news that they might not be "defective" after all. Semester after semester, they sit in slack-jawed horror—tears running down a few faces—as I share Armstrong's thesis and some of the contributing factors that have created the cultural climate for the flourishing of a mental health crisis. For example: is it possible that bigger class size contributes to distractibility in children? How have funding cuts to the arts impacted students? How about the diminish-

---

2. Thomas Armstrong, *The Myth of the A.D.D. Child: 50 Ways to Improve Your Child's Behavior and Attention Span without Drugs, Labels, or Coercion* (New York: Plume, 1997).

ing value of physical education? How has the reframing of kindergarten curriculum—from play based to skill based—impacted the stress levels of young children? Do packaged or fast foods impact the health of our brains? How about sleep or lack of rest? How did our newfound ability, via MRI technology, to "see" brain wave activity contribute to new ideas of normal versus abnormal brain behavior? Did the production of new synthetic drugs intended to impact the brain contribute to an unleashing of new diagnoses? Did the money drug companies could make influence the marketing of "disease?" Is it simply easier to manage a child who doesn't fidget, question, or become disengaged in the classroom? I could go on, but I imagine you get the gist. The bottom line is: *Why do we continually ask what is wrong with our children, rather than what is wrong with our systems of health, education, or families?*

We must think about what our children and our students are trying to tell us with their behavior. In other words, we must put on our proverbial "big-kid" pants and set to work. Could it be that, in the absence of a language of values (Bellah), our children feel confused about appropriate behavior? Is it possible that being born right around 9/11, our children were unduly impacted by our cultural anxiety (Mills)? Across the nation, children who struggle to conform to the demands of our educational system are diagnosed with ADD/ADHD and are medicated into compliance. But what if these disorders are simply the symptoms of an educational system failing to meet the needs of a large number of students and a convenient source of cash for a pharmaceutical industry eager to fill prescriptions (Armstrong)? Where does individual responsibility meet systemic responsibility, and how do these impulses interact?

These are complicated issues. As I like to remind my students, this class is all about peeling back the layers of the artichoke. Eventually, we will get to the heart.

Voting to Volunteering

The day after the 2016 presidential election, there were a lot of long faces among my predominantly liberal students, and, to be honest, I shared their feelings. One of the many things I reflected on that morning was the philosophical underpinnings of our constitution. To be exact, I thought about the connection between "life, liberty, and the pursuit of happiness," three lofty goals eloquently expressed by our founding fathers. This was a moment to remind my students of what we had learned from Bellah and Tocqueville: *the American brand of happiness is literally founded on the principle of engagement.*

So, what happened? Well, I would argue we all got pretty darn wrapped up in ourselves, we lost touch with each other, and we failed to articulate common goals for a fair and just society. As Bellah argued in *Habits of the Heart*, we live in a vastly more interrelated and integrated world—economically, technically, functionally—and yet most of us do not seem to know how to articulate why our lives are morally related to others. We do not think about how our words echo and our actions sting. Importantly, we do not take responsibility for the way our feelings reverberate throughout the atmosphere. This is the flip side of understanding how individual responsibility is related to systemic responsibility: we must recognize that we, as individuals, create the larger system.

In order to help my students shift their perspectives and begin thinking about how taking individual responsibility can change the system, we engaged in the following thought exercise:

Over 120,000,000 people voted in the presidential election. Seventy-six percent of the individuals who voted did so in person. Our guess was that if you consider the commute to the polling location, standing in line, and the act of voting itself, it likely took an average of an hour and a half to get the job done.

We brainstormed a few thoughts regarding this reality:

Voting is the lowest common denominator of true engagement. While voting is important, the true responsibilities of citizenship require engagement beyond an hour-and-a-half commitment. The very nature of voting implies asking someone else to do something for you, rather than figuring out what you can do for yourself and for others.

If those 120,000,000 voters mentioned above offered an hour and a half of time to a constructive volunteer effort once a quarter (which would add up to six hours per year), it would produce 720,000,000 hours of community participation.

Using an eight-hour-a-day model, those hours convert to ninety million workdays. Just imagine what citizens might accomplish if everyone committed to giving six hours of volunteer time a year. Citizenship is not meant to be enacted in isolation. When we limit the benefits of citizenship to voting, passports, and political opinions, we deny ourselves access to the fundamental value of democracy: participation. Furthermore, engagement with the world around us and true connection to other people is what helps us to evolve our consciousness and grow in compassion.

Our behavior is a direct reflection of how we feel. The better we feel, the better we act. The better we act, the better our world becomes. As participating cocreators of reality, we ourselves must take responsibility for ourselves and others by behaving out of a space of well-being and contentment. Shaping new frameworks for thinking, compassion, and kindness will take time. In the end, perhaps, our future will depend not so much on solitary leadership as it will on collective commitment to ourselves and each other. Regaining our footing will require reaching out to each other with trust and a renewed sense of responsibility. We must heal our own hearts. In doing so, we will grow the energy and courage to reach out to others. We will expand our compassion and relinquish our stubborn detachment from others. Finally, our collective healing will return us to the roots of our philosophical ambitions and allow us to "live" the truth of our constitutional rights of life, liberty, and the pursuit of happiness.

Student Paper: Gabriela—A Survivor and an Artist

The events that have played the largest role in developing my identity occurred in my childhood, specifically during the first few years of living in America. My dad's mother had been in Michigan for two decades, and my parents felt the pull of the American dream—they hoped to provide a better future for their daughters and themselves. In May of 2002, the nine of us, including my aunt, uncle, and their children, immigrated to the United States. I had to assimilate to a new society, a new country, and a new home. We moved in with my grandmother and her husband, into a three-bedroom house. I remember learning some conversational phrases, but for the most part, none of us spoke English. I was seven years old.

My parents, aunt, and uncle immediately started working in a factory. They would be gone for twelve-hour shifts, leaving us children alone at home with my grandmother's second husband, K. My parents were gone a lot and were exhausted and distracted when they were home. During those first few weeks, no one noticed that K. was sexually abusing me.

I started second grade and tried to attend the last two months of the school year. I struggled to wrap my mind around all the things that were happening to me. I did not understand what people were saying at school and hated that, but I was terrified to be home with K. Keeping that secret while trying to fit into the American educational system was causing me chronic pain and nausea. I remember going to school only to start feeling hysterical. I would end up calling my mom at work. This caused my parents stress and shame because they would have to ask my Aunt B. for her help translating. My parents made it clear to me that my behavior was irrational. It was their responsibility to go to work every day, so it was my responsibility to go to school, get good grades, and make them proud.

That summer, my cousin and I took English as a Second Language classes and lived with Aunt B. so she could help teach us. I was temporarily removed from K. and the abuse. However, in the fall, my parents were able to buy a house. They endured fourteen-hour work shifts to do so, so my sister and I needed to be watched after school, and K. was a free babysitter. As the abuse continued, I continued to suffer from pain and nausea, and I could not eat.

My parents decided to take me to a doctor, where I was prescribed antinausea medication. After a few weeks of the problem persisting, the doctor voiced her concern that my symptoms were mental manifestations and not physical problems. That night, my parents questioned me about my relationship to K., and I finally told them what had happened. The problem wasn't really resolved. K. denied it, and my grandmother made excuses for him, and blamed me instead. My parents did not want to go to the police. Nothing changed, except K. was not allowed in our house. I still had to see him whenever there was an event at my grandmother's and pretend I was alright.

I formed a series of coping mechanisms to survive through the day. My untreated trauma from the abuse caused me to have symptoms of depression, anxiety, chronic pain, nausea, and dissociation with my body. I felt like a robot, just trying to stay in control of my rage, despair, and pain. I thought that no one cared about my well-being. I did not care about myself. I developed an eating disorder. No one could make me eat, and it finally felt like I had some control of my body. Simultaneously, I knew that this was self-destructive behavior, and I struggled with suicidal thoughts through most of high school.

I felt like my parents expected me to pretend that nothing was wrong. When I brought up that I wanted to go to therapy, they told me to pray for strength and forgiveness. This made me start to doubt the Catholic faith. As a child seeking approval, I stayed quiet most of the time and focused on studying. I knew that as a member of the Polish-American community and the Roman Catholic Church, certain things were expected of me, so I suffered silently. Over the years, it became clearer to me that I did not define my identity with the ideals of these systems of belief. I was distracted by my trauma, and severe anxiety and depression ruled my life and shaped my personality. I did not believe I could be who they told me I should be.

Now that I am older, I can step back and analyze the sociological influences that have affected my personal life and shaped my identity. I think that my parents' decision to be a part of American culture played a large role in the development of who I am. My family has worked hard to ensure a good financial standing. But sometimes, I feel resentment toward my parents, because their pursuit of money was what allowed for K. to abuse me. As a child, I had no control over my situation, and they made decisions about my well-being that influence me to this day. However, I am starting to understand that they were guided by their own social background—the Polish ideology and the Roman Catholic Church—in these decisions. My parents come from a culture that denies sexual abuse and ignores the problem if it does occur. Most families have a similar reaction. Although the exact prevalence is unknown, it is estimated that 12–40 percent of children in the United States experience some form of childhood sexual abuse; shame and stigma prevent many survivors from disclosing abuse (Women's Health Care Physicians). This issue is something that many people face in America, as well as on a larger scale. Sexual abuse and gender- or sexuality-based violence are actually global problems, perhaps the result of the patriarchal and hetero-normative nature of our global society. As somebody that has identified as a victim for a long time, it has helped me to see that it is not just my personal problem, but a public issue that is a big concern. Finally taking a broader look at sexual abuse has validated my feelings. Knowing that others share similar aftereffects of abuse makes me feel normal, like I am not just crazy for feeling the way I do.

Like many people that struggle with anxiety, art became a coping mechanism that helped me gain control of my life in a healthy way. As a child, my parents bought me paint-by-number kits, and I would spend hours meticulously filling in the lines. This soon grew into a skill and appreciation for art. Painting was the therapeutic process that helped me cope with my symptoms. As I got better at art, my self-esteem grew. I developed a sense of self around the persona of the "loner artist." Throughout high school, I used my emotions as the driving force behind my art, and art has helped me gain control of many of my unhealthy coping mechanisms.

Attending college has been a major, life-changing event that has triggered new questions about my identity. When I first came to the College for Creative Studies, I still defined myself as a victim of childhood sexual abuse. I felt lost and unsure about what I was going to do with my life. Sophomore year my awakening began. Since then, I've learned about critical theory, and it opened my eyes to new ideologies. I gained a new understanding of the underlying power structures that rule our daily lives.

The ability to develop the awareness of the power structures present in our lives, which C. Wright Mills calls the "sociological imagination," helps people see the intersection of their own biography with the historical forces that influence their world perspective—resulting in a more self-aware person, who can then effectively shape their place in society. For the majority of my life, I identified as a victim because I thought I would have to face the symptoms of PTSD for the rest of my life. However, when I looked at the broader sociological context surrounding my situation, I realized that it is possible to heal. I have been holding myself back from truly healing by not allowing myself to see past my pain and trauma.

This class gave me the opportunity for introspection and self-analysis. Through meditation, I have expanded my concept of consciousness, of myself, and of my place in society. It has allowed me to be more in tune with myself. As a result, I am now able to acknowledge that my consciousness is separate from my trauma. I had defined myself as a victim, playing the roles of daughter and student, to get through my daily life. Now, I am struggling to regain love and coherence. Only recently have I thought of myself as a survivor and an artist. Letting go of the pain and facing my symptoms will not mean the loss of "myself" but the freedom to be my *true* self, accepting of my past and hopeful about my future.

Oh, Gabriela—

I have sat with your paper for such a long time. I am so very sorry your step-grandfather took advantage of you as a child. The truth is, everyone suffers, but not everyone is able to grow in compassion through their suffering. Some people grow angry, some people just stay sad, and others feel cheated and confused by what they perceive to be the unfairness of life. The wisest among us are able to use their hurt as a vehicle for personal transformation. As the master poet Rumi writes, "We are pain and what cures pain, both. We are the sweet cold water and the jar that pours."[3]

Gabriela, I want to tell you something you might not know about shame: according to psychologists, people who feel shame actually have a heightened sense of self-awareness. Shame stems from our desire to always do our best. And, it results when we feel we are powerless to actualize our best selves. It is the result of feeling vulnerable and helpless, as you did following the abuse you suffered and your parents' unwillingness to truly acknowledge it. Shame is closely related to guilt—but while guilt is related to not meeting someone else's expectations, shame is related to a failure to meet our own expectations. In other words, shame is a result of letting yourself down. Forgive yourself for letting your trauma define you for so long, Gabriela—you were a sweet little girl who was taken advantage of in an act of cruelty and dysfunction. It's OK—you didn't do anything wrong, and you developed the best coping mechanisms you could at the time.

The truth is, we are sometimes limited in our knowing—but never limited in our capacity to learn. I admire your honest reflections on your family life. And I am sorry you were hurt by them. But your paper shows strong evidence that you are moving past these memories and recognizing the power of the lessons embedded in these interactions.

You are truly a beautiful writer—your words shine a light on your insight and evolving spirit. You write that learning that others suffer from similar aftereffects of abuse helped you realize that you are not "just crazy" for feeling the way you do. No—you are not. We are simply not given enough room in our modern culture to explore these negative experiences and how they shape our lives. Sometimes when an individual is forced to fit into society by conforming to social ideals, their emotions become suppressed and they lose touch with their own authentic being

---

3. Rumi, *The Essential Rumi*, trans. Coleman Barks with John Moyne (New York: Harper Collins, 1995), 106.

as well as their innate knowledge of the universe at large. This is why I am such a firm believer in connecting students with the underpinnings of their stories. It helps them to see themselves as whole and resilient.

Appreciation can change my whole semester—thank you for validating my curriculum as meaningful. The example of your ongoing transformation will become my fuel for the next semesters. As the Dalai Lama wrote, "The roots of all goodness lie in the soil of appreciation for goodness."[4]

Thank you for your raw honesty, Gabriela. I was very moved by your story—it was truly an honor to read your words and to witness your strength in the face of such adversity. Congratulations on graduating—I think you have much to look forward to. I am excited to watch your journey unfold from the sidelines. I will hold you in my heart and wish you continued healing . . .

Much love,

Molly

---

4. Dalai Lama, *The Path to Enlightenment*, trans. and ed. Glenn H. Mullin (Shambala, 1994), 105.

Seventh Week

What Do We Really Learn in School?

The academy is not paradise. But learning is a place where paradise can be created. The classroom, with all its limitations, remains a location of possibility. In that field of possibility we have the opportunity to labor for freedom, to demand of ourselves and our comrades, an openness of mind and heart that allows us to face reality even as we collectively imagine ways to move beyond boundaries, to transgress. This is education as the practice of freedom.

—bell hooks

Kindergarten as Academic Boot Camp

One of my most vivid memories of childhood happened during my kindergarten year. I specifically remember sitting cross-legged on a brightly colored rug watching my teacher, Mrs. Allen, flip the pages of an oversized book of letters. A is for Apple, B is for Book, and so on. Given the fact that I came to school knowing my letters, I would get so bored during this activity. I can remember jiggling my legs in an effort to make the time move faster.

One day I wore a red-and-white checkered dress with buttons all the way down the front. To ease my boredom on this particular day, I began to button and unbutton all those little buttons up and down my dress. In my distracted mood, I accidently unbuttoned my dress all the way to the top! I don't think anyone noticed, but I can distinctly remember feeling utterly horrified by my mistake. It was a moment that taught me the risks of daydreaming in school. Heaven forbid you lose track of yourself, you might end up embarrassing yourself beyond redemption. I didn't learn anything new about the alphabet, but I learned about the type of behavior that was expected of me.

My students are often surprised to realize that much of their early schooling was about understanding behavioral expectations, not about learning how to learn. Do you remember what you learned in kindergarten? Most likely, you learned how to sit still, how to be quiet, how to follow instructions, how to share with others, and how to line up in a neat little row. One article that explores these themes in a most effective way is "Kindergarten as Academic Boot Camp."[1] Written several decades ago by Harry Gracey, the article feels a bit outdated and old-fashioned. That said, few readings or discussions elicit as much heated conversation in my class as this one. Gracey's recounting of a typical kindergarten day offers a template of understanding that no theoretical mumbo-jumbo could ever convey. During the day Gracey observed and describes, the kindergarten teacher repeatedly ignores questions from curious students about anything vaguely "off-topic," cuts the students off in the midst of acts of creative invention and pretending in favor of sticking to the timetable, and requires the students to follow her instructions without explaining why, even when they ask. Reading this article is a bit like getting cold water thrown on your face. Gracey's main message is that school is really about training individuals to be obedient to authority. This is a big wake-up call for most students. Honestly, this article just totally gets under my students' skin in an awakening kind of way.

Reprimand as Assault

Initially, my students' reaction to the Gracey article surprised and humored me. I couldn't quite believe that it had never occurred to them that a large part of the learning experience was tied to understanding behavioral expectations. Over time, however, I began to see that my students were not outraged by the imposition of rules and routines in the kindergarten classroom. In fact, they acknowledge the necessity of creating structure.

---

1. Harry Gracey, "Kindergarten as Academic Boot Camp," in *Sociology: A Down-to-Earth Approach, 12th Edition*, edited by James M. Henslin (London: Pearson, 2013), 390–404.

Their frustration lay in the method of communication used by the teacher in the article and, more importantly, the teachers of their collective memories.

It seems that many students "hear" behavioral reprimands as personal critique. Rather than understanding the teacher's words as an attempt to engage them in the routine of the classroom, students interpret reprimands as personal assaults. This severely impacts their developing self-esteem and, more importantly, pushes them to the outside edge of the communal classroom. Over time, children who interpret behavioral reprimands as personal assaults begin to feel isolated, misunderstood, and alienated from the larger classroom experience.

I have thought a lot about why some children "hear" behavioral reprimands as personal assaults. I can only come up with one hypothesis: children are generally much better at reading the undercurrent of emotionality than adults realize. A teacher may be saying in words, "Sit still, Johnny," but Johnny is *feeling* her say, "Johnny, you are making me nuts." Johnny is ultimately experiencing rejection from the very person attempting to engage him in the learning process.

We know that classroom success leads to self-confidence. How does a young child grow his self-confidence when he experiences feelings of rejection in the classroom? It doesn't matter if the rejection is real or imagined, the perception is what impacts the child. Teaching is an inter-actional process. Every thought, word, and action produces an influence in the classroom atmosphere. The feeling of that atmosphere is dependent on the quality of the emotions flowing through the teacher. As a result, a teacher with love in his or her heart will establish a more loving and nurturing classroom experience. As Jim Henson, the creative genius behind the Muppets, once said, "[Kids] don't remember what you try to teach them. They remember what you are."[2]

Being a teacher carries with it great potential and great obligation. The current education landscape has as yet no socially based accountability for classroom etiquette. According to my students, teachers would do well to monitor their own stress levels in the classroom, communicate with love in their hearts, and understand that children can feel the emotional vibrations beneath their words.

---

2. Jim Henson, *It's Not Easy Being Green: And Other Things to Consider* (Glendale, CA: Kingswell, 2005).

A Different Type of Classroom

A classroom can become a space for healing from the early trauma of behavioral conditioning. I create a nurturing environment in which students feel safe and confident about volunteering their ideas or asking questions. I do not require students to take notes if they prefer to simply sit and listen; I trust them to know how they learn best. In an atmosphere of encouragement and support, without fear of being reprimanded, young people blossom and focus on learning.

My curriculum also integrates a five-hour experiential module devoted to meditation training. For the first several semesters of my course, my students learned Transcendental Meditation. (Full disclosure: I am a long-time TM meditator.) TM is a mantra-based meditation practice taught by professionally trained teachers over the course of about six hours of instruction. After a few semesters, however, I decided to incorporate Deepak Chopra's Primordial Sound Technique. It too is taught by professionally trained teachers. This change was implemented due to cost considerations and the availability of local teachers. My students have enjoyed both techniques (see appendix). After the training is complete, we meditate together for twenty minutes in the middle of each three-hour class. The rest of the class is devoted to traditional academic lecture and discussions.

The curriculum I teach is not about navel gazing or tree hugging—although I encourage both activities in time away from the classroom! All of my experience as an educator and parent has led me to conclude that a sense of reverence is necessary for the health of our students. If a culture is devoid of reverence, we deny ourselves inspiration. The entire experience of education should be about the art of awakening the natural curiosity of the students we have the honor of teaching. The job of the teacher is to make tangible the inner workings of the mind.

Consciousness-centered education brings the inner and outer—subjective and objective—worlds closer together. When we are able to see beyond the gross level, we are able to connect with the pulsing urges that exist beneath the surface of known reality. This is where all the ideas live. Unencumbered by the weight of our stress, we can dive deep into this bubbling pool of knowledge and creativity. As Daniel Barbezat and Mirabai Bush write in their book, *Contemplative Practices in Higher Education: Powerful Methods to Transform Teaching and Learning*, "Contemplative and introspective modes of learning are an exciting pedagogical development. Placing students at the heart of their education fosters a rich environment for learning and provides the opportunity for students to cultivate attention, deepen their understanding of their studies, engender richer relationships with themselves and others, and stimulate profound inquiries into the nature of themselves and the world around them."[3]

It is not my claim that every class needs to include a meditation practice. Nor do I simply advance mantra-based meditation—specifically in the form of Transcendental or Primordial Sound—as the only gateway to obtaining silence. There are a multitude of meditation techniques supported by evidence-based research that have been shown to reduce stress and anxiety, increase creativity, lower blood pressure, enhance self-confidence, and so on. Providing meditation training to my students is simply my effort to take responsibility as a teacher.

One of my "bibles" is Mary Rose O'Reilly's classic, *The Peaceable Classroom.*[4] In this tender and heartfelt book, O'Reilly poses the question of whether or not it is possible to "teach English so that people stop killing each other?"[5] Later, she writes, "Critical thinking has traditionally involved stating the merits of something, stating its weaknesses, contextualizing it in a tradition, and comparing it to others of its kind—all necessary operations of culture. But what I'd like to see is more balance. Mostly we are taught and encouraged to find fault. In academic culture, the one who is the most negative is often considered the most intellectual. What's going on here? We are rewarding sick, perverse, poisonous behavior. We should stop promoting these people and simply set them to making commercials for breakfast cereals."[6] Providing my students with the opportunity to learn to meditate from a professionally trained teacher is simply my response to O'Reilly's call to action.

Integrating meditation into the core curriculum of an academic class nurtures my students in unexpected ways. There is a lovely intimacy that

---

3. Daniel P. Barbezat and Mirabai Bush, *Contemplative Practices in Higher Education: Powerful Methods to Transform Teaching and Learning* (San Francisco: Jossey-Bass, 2014), 20.

4. Mary Rose O'Reilly, *The Peaceable Classroom* (Portsmouth, NH: Boynton/Cook, 1993).

5. O'Reilly, *The Peaceable Classroom*, 9.

6. O'Reilly, *The Peaceable Classroom*, 92.

is created in the mere act of closing your eyes with a group of people. The "experiment" offers students the chance to learn, for one semester, in a relaxed atmosphere. Rather than distract from objective learning goals, meditating together encourages lively conversation. It also offers my students and me permission to just "be" together in a nonjudgmental way. It is my hope that sharing my story will offer other educators encouragement to think outside of the box in their efforts to create peaceable classrooms across the country.

Two Student Paper Responses: Different Students Have Different Needs

Over the years, there has been increased pressure from my department chair to develop a standardized grading rubric. In certain ways, rubrics really ease the complexity of grading. They also ensure that particular learning expectations are being met by students. Rubrics also keep me disciplined, reminding me not to be distracted by every potential conversational offshoot. There are certain assignments that call for a strong rubric.

The problem with rubrics, however, is they frequently limit flexibility to evaluate according to particular individual skill and effort. The following two letters serve as case in point.

The first letter was sent to a student who essentially "mailed it in." Ashley's work was emblematic of a paper written by a traditionally successful student. Too often, students who have successfully conquered the rubric learn how to write only what is expected. While they have academic confidence and intellectual skill, they often they lack curiosity, motivation, and, frankly, integrity of effort.

The second letter was written to Liz, a young woman with a learning disability. I have many students with learning disabilities, writing anxiety, and the general weaknesses that come from attending a lesser-quality high school. Ironically, I find that these students are often some of my strongest students. They are hungry for success, motivated by their desire to be seen, and often significantly more creative thinkers.

I happened to have a soft spot in my heart for both of these young women. They were particularly earnest in their reflections. Writing back to students like Liz and Ashley is nuanced. Their papers reveal radically different approaches. Both papers, however, received the same grade: B+.

Ashley—The Most Frustrating Type of Student

Dear Ashley—

You are the kind of student that frustrates me. Let me explain. I find teaching at CCS to be a remarkable experience. CCS students, on the whole, are wise, insightful, irreverent, and creative. I find that they are generally interested in ideas but not so interested in academia. I mean, I get it. They came to art school to have more freedom of expression, to spend time in the studio—not to be bogged down with a bunch of research papers. Believe me, it can be a real challenge to strike the right balance in a liberal arts class. Sometimes, I feel like a dog and pony show! You know, the truth is—drumroll, please—I happen to like academia. I like to read. I love the challenge of stringing together ideas and seeing the patterns come to life using the written word. Academic writing is an art form. Certainly, it doesn't resonate with everyone, but neither does ceramics.

You are a writer—a good writer. "Education is a structured vehicle for imprinting culture and its morality onto the young and malleable youth of society, meant to train children for future generations of progress in the same unwavering direction." Wow. Here is the issue: while your paper is good—one of the very best in the class—it is not nearly as good as it could be. You have barely scratched the surface of *your ability* to evaluate culture. The truth is, you have done exactly what I asked the class to do and nothing more. I should have written a separate assignment for you.

You have a naturally evaluative mind. You are curious about the way the world works and capable of seeing the many layers of contrast between what is inherently moral and what our societal belief systems tell us is the truth. This fact makes your voice powerful. I feel cheated at the end of your paper because I feel like I didn't get to see a whole lot of Ashley. I want more, more, more!

In his paper, Steven makes some very wise comments about humor, happiness, and depth. He writes about the ultimate goal being to just feel happy. I agree with him. Here's the deal: if you truly understand and embody the rules, expectations, and routines of society, you are better able to achieve freedom than one who does not. This may sound ironic but it is true. I will share with you the same story from Maharishi that I shared with Steve: there are two ways to discipline a dog. If you tie the dog to a leash in the yard and run after it every time it gets out of the yard, the dog will do everything in its power to escape. If you don't tie the dog up or run after it when it leaves the yard, but instead let the dog come and go as it pleases and simply put some food it likes outside the door, the dog will become a faithful friend who's always at your door. You will have control over the dog without forcefully controlling it. It's similar when we want to discipline the mind; the easier method is to not restrain it or try to control it. The mind is drawn to happiness; if you lead it toward happiness, it will stay there through its own desire for happiness.

I happen to really resonate with your stop-motion work. The use of a Pegasus as the hero of your story is so brilliant! There is depth there—in the silliness and fun of the story. Not everyone can do that, Ashley. You write: "Growing up, I was quite fearful of being labeled a 'bad kid.'" Later you write: "Good and bad bled together: black and white mixed to make infinite shades of gray." Bingo! Makes you wonder if the universe ultimately has an opinion on good and bad or just stands aside and lets us work to figure it out—sometimes lots of good comes from an initially bad decision, and some bad can come from an initially good one. Understanding the mechanics of structure helps one to make the best decisions and move with a sense of grace and automation.

You don't have to be any which way, Ashley. You can be an academic writer and a silly girl filled with humor and depth and insight. I am starting to ramble but I just really want to stress to you that I appreciate your rule-following, good-girl self AND your irreverence. I see your depth AND your silliness. I value your inquisitive mind AND your desire to just have fun. You got it all, girlfriend. It has been a real pleasure getting to know you this semester.

Love,

Molly

Liz—Teeter-Totter Confidence

Oh, beautiful Liz—

You describe a pretty rough ride—and one that I understand personally. My hunch is you have a pretty special mama—one who suffered with you but remained strong in her commitment to support your growth by making you get out there and try it again. This is not an easy task—watching your child suffer is profoundly painful. All you want to do is protect the fragile heart—but good moms know that children get stronger by facing challenges and learning how to operate in a society that isn't always accepting of difference.

Your description of living with a learning disability is beautiful in its raw honesty. You describe the consequences on your self-esteem so well: "I was picked on by other students because I was 'stupid.' My teachers and tutors made the point over and over again by placing me in low-rated groups. It did not help me learn; instead it helped other students to recognize me as different. The confidence I felt as a young child living in a loving family just slipped away slowly over time." It's tough to put in a dollar and consistently get ten cents back—especially when you have such a rich inner landscape. It's also got to be tremendously frustrating to be offered so few ways to validate your own inner knowingness.

For what it's worth, I want you to know that I "see" you. I know how hard you work. And, importantly, the intelligence of an open, empathic heart is the greatest gift anyone can offer to society. Just you wait for the world to catch up, Liz. Growing your self-confidence, finding like-minded friends, and staying committed to your passions/talents will bring you success and validation. Promise.

I shared the following story with another student in class. I think it fits here too. This is the story of one of my very favorite parenting moments. Now, in truth, it is also a moment of "delinquency" that I never would have encouraged—however, the sweet feeling of graceful revenge filled my heart with pride. My middle daughter, Cami, also got off to a late start. She was a "slow" learner—diagnosed with ADD/ADHD, put in slow math and reading groups, etc. She too suffered at the hands of insensitive teachers—so many stories of being dismissed, unseen, misunderstood, etc. Of course, she didn't help the situation much—much of the time during middle school she felt like a Coke can that has been shaken, fizzing with anger. I was strict—didn't let her get away with much. It was hard for me, as my nature is to want to have fun together. I think Cami had twenty-two detentions freshman year of high school—mostly for stuff like dropping her pencil in class, walking out of the room without asking, wearing her skirt too short (she went to Catholic school—lots of opportunities to get in trouble for dumb stuff! It was good for her. She needed to act out in small ways because she was pissed at being so misunderstood.)

Anyway, my favorite moment came during graduation. Cami's grade point average kept her near the bottom of her class. She didn't win any awards and wasn't viewed as a successful "star" of the class. The afternoon of graduation, she went to Michaels and bought two cords—one blue and one yellow. They looked exactly like the cords the honor students wore at graduation. She wore them proudly across the stage as her own personal mark of success. When she reached the principal on stage, he glanced at her, taking in the cords immediately. Even he had to smile. It was a triumphant moment of victory. And, a reminder that all of us must find ways to validate our own knowingness.

You asked for some help connecting your story back to the readings. I have a few ideas:

In the article "Kindergarten as Academic Boot Camp," Harry Gracey says that schooling is ultimately meant to train students for "conformity." In the third paragraph of your paper, when you talk about your early experiences in school, you could add a sentence or two about how the pressure to conform impacts students with learning disabilities. Then, you could list two or three specific ways that teachers could have done things differently to help you learn in a style that worked for you. Do you think growing up in a cultural context that celebrated your learning differences rather than insisting you conform would have alleviated your suffering?

As we discussed in class, C. Wright Mills is a good reference to use in the paper. As he suggests, neither the life of an individual nor the history of a society can be understood without contemplating both. In the fourth paragraph of your paper, you write about how your experiences of not being a "successful" student influenced every other aspect of your life: "I loved sports but I never had the confidence to play well on a team. I attracted the wrong kind of boys and didn't believe I was deserving of a nice boy." This would be a good place to add a quote from C. Wright Mills about the sociological imagination and to reflect on the bigger cultural picture: What types of messages do we receive from our culture about "success" in general? Why do you think that a person who is not "successful" in school feels she cannot be successful in the rest of her life?

In *The Book of Secrets*, Deepak Chopra writes, "Reality is perception, and the suffering person gets trapped by negative perceptions of his own creation. Perception keeps the pain under control, not by reducing it but by sealing out even greater pain."[7] The places where we hurt are generally where we "lock" our perception. Why don't you include a paragraph on how meditation has helped you to unlock your perception that your learning disability defined you? You write about that quite eloquently in the first paragraph by talking about how "you" are separate from your experiences: "Learning to meditate this semester has helped me more than I could ever have imagined. Meditation helped me to see, feel, and know my internal goodness as separate from my experiences." You could expand on that theme by describing the first moment you realized that "you" are not simply your learning disability—was it during meditation or during some other moment in your life? It would be interesting to describe that moment and how it made you feel. Was it one big realization, or a series of small ones? It would also be interesting to add a few sentences about how this realization has changed your daily life and your attitude about it.

You'll notice that I've made some corrections to grammar, spelling, and punctuation throughout your paper. I recognize the challenge that writing presents for students with learning

---

7. Deepak Chopra, *The Book of Secrets* (London: Ebury Publishing, 2009), 67.

disabilities. The mechanics of writing can take a long time to learn, so be patient with yourself. You have clearly worked very hard on your writing, and you have every reason to feel proud and to assume that your writing will continue to improve.

I have a beautiful garden in my backyard. The woman who helped me plan it made it clear that we needed to have a diversity of flowers in the bed. We laughed a lot during the planning— you see, I happen to really love lilies and other July-blooming flowers. Debra reminded me that I wanted a garden that flowered throughout the year. And, she was right. In the spring, I have tulips and daffodils, in the summer I enjoy my lilies, in the fall I have mums, and in the winter, berries. There is a season for every kind of blossom. Children, like flowers, should never be rushed. Your paper shows that with care and time and self-awareness, everyone can blossom: "My confidence continues to grow. Art school has helped. I'm actually a really talented photographer. I've even won some awards. I am beginning to understand that life is a process." I am so happy I got to meet you in your blooming season!

Much love,

Molly

Eighth Week

How Do We Know What We Know?

Some Questions You Might Ask

Is the soul solid, like iron?
Or is it tender and breakable, like
The wings of a moth in the beak of the owl?
Who has it, and who doesn't?
I keep looking around me.
The face of the moose is as sad
As the face of Jesus.
The swan opens her white wings slowly.
In the fall, the black bear carries leaves into the darkness.
One question leads to another.
Does it have a shape? Like an iceberg?
Like the eye of a hummingbird?
Does it have one lung, like the snake and the scallop?
Why should I have it, and not the anteater?
Who loves her children?
Why should I have it, and not the camel?
Come to think of it, what about the maple trees?
What about the blue iris?
What about all the little stones, sitting alone in the moonlight?
What about roses and lemons, and their shining leaves?
What about the grass?

—Mary Oliver

What Is It Like to Be a Bat?

Can you imagine how it would feel to perceive the world with a bat's senses, with a bat's mind? Bats navigate the world using echolocation, using hearing

as their primary sense. They are nocturnal. Oh, yes, and they can fly. Bats'
sensory experiences are completely at odds with our human experiences.
We can't fly, we understand the world most immediately through vision,
we can't echolocate, and we like to sleep when it's dark. How, then, can
a human possibly imagine what it feels like to live as a bat?

Thomas Nagel used this thought experiment in his 1974 philosophical work, "What Is It Like to Be a Bat,"[1] to prove that the entire
idea of understanding the essence of another's experiences is so difficult
to comprehend that to even make people think about it, he must ask a
"trick" question. His point is that comments on an experience are, by
nature, always subjective—in other words, from your own point of view.
The whole idea of an objective account, therefore, makes no sense. As the
old Native American adage goes, "To understand a man, you must first
walk a mile in his moccasins."

Nagel wrote during a time that physicalist arguments, which reduce
the mental to the merely physical, were becoming a formidable front in
the investigation of consciousness. Medical breakthroughs in the late '60s
and '70s were offering doctors pictures of the brain for the first time. The
question, of course, was what do those pictures tell us? The notion that all
human behavior would be explainable through understanding brain activity
was creating quite a buzz in neuroscience circles. Nagel's work challenged
this new trend by calling attention to the ways in which our experience
of consciousness cannot be objectively measured or perceived. Thus, he
made a very strong case for the phenomenon of conscious experience
having subjective meaning.

In later work, Nagel goes much farther in his discussion of the irreducible nature of human experience and the relevance of subjectivity. The
title of his 2012 book offers a not-so-subtle hint regarding the progression
of his thinking: *Mind and Cosmos: Why the Materialist Neo-Darwinism
Conception of Nature Is Almost Certainly False*. In this book, Nagel argues
"that the mind-body problem is not just a local problem . . . it invades our
understanding of the entire cosmos and its history."[2] While Nagel's theories
remain on the cutting edge, he offers us a gateway to a very important

---

1. Thomas Nagel, "What Is It Like to Be a Bat?," *Philosophical Review* 84, no. 4 (October
1974): 435–50. doi:10.2307/2183914.

2. Thomas Nagel, *Mind and Cosmos: Why the Materialist Neo-Darwinian Conception
of Nature Is Almost Certainly False* (Oxford: Oxford University Press, 2012), 3.

conversation about the irreducible nature of the human experience and the relevance of subjectivity.

The Danger of Answers

Can we describe the experience of being conscious? How do we understand the difference between our subjective and objective experiences in the world? Does language constrain our ability to explain the fullness of experience? Is the world we perceive to be "real" actually illusory?

Most of the learning that happens on a day-to-day basis operates automatically, spontaneously, and without instruction. We navigate our lives feeling by feeling. It's so natural we don't recognize the process as unique or special. It just is. This phenomenon—our subjective experience—influences our knowing at every level. Feeling colors knowing. It may be abstract, difficult to define, and amorphous, but feeling ultimately drives experience.

What is beneath the level of feeling? Well, this is where things get tricky. We are perceivers. We tend to spend our time on the surface level of our perceptions and sensations. This is understandable. In fact, throughout the history of human thought, humans have endeavored to understand the universe as related to ourselves and to our own *experiences in waking life* of ourselves. Certainly, understanding in terms of the wee little self makes sense, as it is what we have at our disposal. But is it possible to move beyond individual knowing and into the realm of unified knowing?

The great philosophers and writers of the Age of Enlightenment certainly thought so. According to Edward O. Wilson, "The Enlightenment quest was driven by the belief that entirely on their own, human beings can know all that needs to be known, and in knowing understand, and in understanding gain power to choose more wisely than ever before."[3] This idea that human beings might be able to know all that needs to be known through reason and logic alone is appealing. But it only tells part of the story. True learning is grounded in subjective understanding and in the deeper experiences of the spirit. When intellectual life is supported by a deep intuition and contentment, its functioning becomes creative,

---

3. Edward O. Wilson, *The Meaning of Human Existence* (New York: Liveright Publishing, 2014), 38.

fruitful, and significant instead of barren, ineffective, and meaningless. We must find ways to look inward as well as outward.

This realm of inward investigation, long sidelined in Western thought, has been a focus of Eastern philosophies for millennia. These traditions have long accepted that we must learn to transcend the thinking mind and sensation in order to experience fullness. This entails moving beyond the finite experience of individuality into the infinite experience of consciousness. We do this by silencing the mind through meditation.

Buddha refers to this experience as "no-self." It refers to an utter emptiness, nothingness, no thingness. The question arises: When thoughts cease, who are you? In other words, Buddha says that when mind ceases, there is no self left. Without mind, you become universal, you overflow the boundaries of the ego. You become pure space, uncontaminated by anything at all. Some call this the experience of becoming a mirror that reflects nothing.

The process of transcending is characterized by experiencing sensation on progressively subtler levels of the mind. As we transcend the sensation, we arrive at the infinitely more settled, blissful source of said sensation. A meditation teacher I used to know described the sensation of transcending sight the following way: he would ask students to imagine we were viewing a train moving away from us toward the horizon. There comes a moment when we are aware of the most subtle form of the train at the horizon, and then it slips away, and we are aware of the expanse of the horizon itself, or the sun setting—poof! And only the light remains.

A few semesters ago, I had a student named Jacob who shared a wonderful story about visiting the Smithsonian Air and Space Museum as a child. During his summertime visit, he spontaneously reached out to touch an old airplane. He wrote:

"Touching that plane remains the most pivotal moment of my life. For this one second, I could feel the motion embodied in that fantastic machine. I could hear it in the air. I felt connected to its mission in this unexplainable, profound way. It's like I knew that plane. Even writing about the experience now gives me chills. To be honest, I never even told my parents. The whole episode only lasted a moment. It felt so crazy—like an out-of-body experience. I didn't know how to explain it—to myself or anyone else for that matter. I don't know, maybe it was my childish runaway imagination working overtime. But I swear to you, it's the moment that propelled me to design school. The idea of creating something that could contain that kind of energy and history just totally overwhelmed and inspired me from that instant on."

Could it be that Jacob experienced a moment of transcendent unity with the plane? Is it possible that his innocent curiosity transcended time and space in a way that allowed him to feel all the subtle layers of creation that made up the existence of that airplane? Is it possible that the energy of all those people who made that plane, flew that plane, and rode in that plane still resides within that plane? For that matter, is it possible that the plane has an identity? An identity that pulses to be seen, to be known, to connect? I don't know the answers to any of these questions. But is it possible that investigating our silent selves might reveal additional answers to the question "how do we know what we know?"

Every semester, I tell my students that the goal of my class is to have them leave the semester knowing less. This confuses them terribly. In our culture, it is no easy task to accept that we may not know everything. One unintended by-product of the information age is that it can be very difficult to hear anything as new, distinct, or interesting. There is just a tsunami of information rolling toward the beach every freaking day. Information changes so fast and moves so rapidly, it's tough to distinguish what to attend to. It's like having the Charlie Brown droning teacher voice as the backdrop to your every waking moment. Google search bars at the tip of our fingers ensure that we must have an answer for every question. But what if we are actually asking the wrong questions? Or, as the Greeks proposed, what if we do not even know what we don't know?

Too often in academia, we use theory and science as information to be conquered rather than integrated. We create unnecessary boundaries between the knower and the known. This practice creates a separation between teachers and students and, importantly, between what is known and what needs to be known. It is in this space that students begin to invent information to fill in the blanks. This is a dangerous practice, as it encourages reliance on belief rather than fact. The classroom becomes a space to confirm what we believe rather than acknowledge what we don't know. Belief is an amorphous category that often produces needless worry, a reliance on myth, and the invention of "alternative facts," which can be dangerous. Getting to the bottom of the impact of belief is tricky business. It helps to start with the awareness that all knowledge comes from questions we ask. It is only possible to find answers when we are comfortable admitting what we don't know.

Evidence of the Underpinnings of the Invisible

Several years ago while on vacation in Amsterdam, my husband bought me a thin ring encrusted with seed diamonds to be worn stacked with my engagement ring and wedding band. One day shortly after he gave it to me, it accidently slipped off my finger. After spending several days retracing my steps, cleaning out my car, and calling all the spots I had visited, I accepted the fact that it was probably gone for good.

About a week later, I had the oddest dream. In fact, it was so strange it woke me out of a deep, deep sleep and left me buzzing with curiosity. In the dream, a man was painting the interior walls of my house. He was a colorful character, essentially dancing through my home swinging his arms in an elegant fashion. The images he produced were totally entrancing. The most amazing aspect, however, was that he did not have a paintbrush! Everywhere he went, beautiful imagery just flowed out of his being. It was as if he had entered my dreamscape to remind of the magic in the world.

The next morning was one of those crisp, cold, Michigan blue-sky days. My husband and son were out in the yard raking leaves. I was at the kitchen sink washing the breakfast dishes. Suddenly, I heard Mike yell, "Molly, come quick!" When I walked outside, he pointed to my ring sitting innocently on the post rail of our side porch. It looked as if it had been gently placed there by invisible hands. It was missing one diamond.

Ever since that morning, I have worn that ring snugly between my wedding band and my engagement ring. I have never replaced the missing diamond. I wear it as a constant reminder of my belief that to all things visible there is also the invisible. For most people, "real" is what they interact with every day. It is what they think about, what they "know," and what they can trust. And yet there have always been people in every culture who possess the ability to cross invisible thresholds into the unseen. In fact, I think most of us operate with this gnawing sense at the edge of our awareness that what we "see" is only part of the story.

I pass my ring around the classroom while I share this story. I don't insist that the man from my dream brought the ring back to me. I allow the possibility, however, to hover in the air. Last semester, one young woman said, "Oh, Molly, I love your story! Today while driving to class, I drove through a beautiful storm of swirling dogwood petals. It felt like I was crossing into a new, magical dimension! I'm thinking I might use the experience as inspiration for a short film I am putting together. You've given me the courage to think it might be a good idea!"

There is a certain risk in sharing the story of the disappearance of my ring and its magical return on the pages of an "academic" book. I recognize that I may be setting myself up to be perceived as a charlatan. Any movement away from grading rubrics, learning outcomes, and evidence-based teaching represents a threat to accreditation boards, department heads, and the assembly-line-style learning system that we have come to recognize as productive. It is a risk I am willing to take.

Every day and in so many ways we are offered evidence of the underpinnings of the invisible—the wind, gravity, our intuition, every abstract idea we have ever pondered. And yet, so often, we deny the magic. In my mind, an adherence to accepting only the concrete vision of what one can see, hear, touch, feel, or understand limits one's ability to grow in wisdom. A "figure it out," evaluative mentality limits our imagination. It is impossible for the finite mind to begin to understand the complexities of the universe.

Student Paper: Olivia—Analysis Paralysis

Last semester around the end of March, I changed places for about five days. Against my better judgment, I took a flight to Miami to attend a music festival during one of the most demanding months of school. I knew I would be exhausted beyond repair when I got back, but it didn't matter. Despite the fact that my friends backed out of the trip at the last minute, I decided to forge ahead on my own.

Ironically, the strain that led to my need to escape was not so much an overload of assignments or the stress of sitting in class. It was the required "critical thinking" demanded by my professors. The constant need to justify my ideas by finding heaps of supporting evidence. While I generally enjoy the challenge of academic work, the pattern of critical thinking that is supposed to be tied solely to my life as a student had organically seeped into my every waking moment. By the time March had arrived, I desperately needed to regain some balance.

The Oxford Dictionary defines escapism as "the tendency to seek distraction and relief from unpleasant realities, especially by seeking entertainment or engaging in fantasy."[4] My guess is that spontaneously

---

4. Definition of "escapism," Oxford Dictionaries website, accessed October 24, 2018, https://en.oxforddictionaries.com/definition/escapism.

leaving town for a music festival in Miami probably qualifies as a pretty healthy "escapist" choice.

The festival broke my mind-set by offering a mental revival of sorts. In addition to breaking my "analysis paralysis," the festival reinvigorated my spirit by reminding me to laugh and dance, live in the moment, and feel my own true essence as an individual capable of navigating time and space independent of the crutch that is evaluation. Critical thinking be damned! I felt free!

Inherent to the definition of escapism is the need to run from the reality of our day-to-day existence. An escapist identity is celebrated in the cultural context through our books, movies, advertising, and, ironically, through our obsession with reality TV. We run from our tendencies, our lives, our mistakes, our decisions, our families, what we can and cannot control.

During Christmas vacation the year I was twelve, my entire existence was reset by an event completely beyond my control. My uncle, grandmother, and three young cousins were murdered. While wrapping Christmas gifts the evening before the discovery of this horrific event, I had experienced an unfamiliar feeling of anxiety. I sometimes reflect on that moment. It makes me wonder about the energetic connection between people and events.

To develop the skill of living in the moment, we must release our fantasy of behaving as an escape artist. For me, the pull toward escape is constant. The ironic reality, however, is that no matter how far I run, I find I take myself with me. The subtle presence of all I yearn to escape from always simmers just beneath the surface of my thinking mind. Strangely, the pressure at school to engage in constant critical thinking moves me away from feeling my truth. Escaping allows me to feel the moment-to-moment engagement with the emotional landscape that is my private sanctuary of grief. It is in this space that I can regain some connection to the love that remains as a soft, subtle connection to all I have lost. It is in that space that I can remind myself to choose to move forward rather than simply burying the totality of who I am.

Dear Olivia—

Where to begin? Your paper was the first paper I read last December. It moved me so deeply that I could not read another for several days. I am so sorry for your profound, unimaginable loss. I have sat several times to write you a paper response.

Words, however, feel like an inadequate response. At any rate, I woke this morning feeling the pull of your spirit and knowing that I needed to respond to your paper.

Your reference to "escapism" is intriguing. I understand why a trip to Miami—during midterm week—felt like a taking the exit ramp from real life. And, yet, your reflections on the experience reveal a return to the real YOU in a rich and meaningful way. How ironic that you needed to get out of the "critical-thinking world" to return to the "living-in-the-moment world." I am sure that trip fed your soul in ways unimaginable—reminding you of why you like being alive, being with people, and feeling good. The escapism you crave is not to get away from yourself, but to get back to yourself!

Once we become aware of the forces working to condition our thinking, we can begin to surrender some of the hold those forces have over us. In this case, the enormity of the pressure to remain in critical-thinking mode was distorting your experience of yourself. Denying you access to the river of feeling that runs through you continually upholding your sense of self.

Years ago during a difficult time in my life, a good and wise friend gave me some useful advice. Deb works as a spiritual advisor and health coach. I trust her implicitly, as she offers both practical advice and healing compassion. On the afternoon I called to share my woes with her, she listened intently and with great patience. After telling my story—in the moment just before she shared her response—there was a sweet, pregnant moment of silence. Somehow, I knew that very moment contained all the potential answers to my prayers. And, do you know what Deb said to me, Olivia? She said, in a deeply serious, reverent voice, "Oh, Molly, you really need to get out and have some fun!"

"What!*&^%&^!!!" my mind screamed in rage and frustration. "Are you kidding me, fun?! Did she hear a word of my story?"

It was about a week later that I found myself at the grocery store. Still feeling the strain of my sorrows, the notion of planning yet another dinner filled me with despair. Watching the people shop around me, carefully picking out fruits and veggies, I felt so overwhelmed by the mundane nature of life. And, it was in that moment, out of the corner of my eye, that I caught sight of something I had never noticed in all my years of grocery shopping: egg-roll sheets. It was as if my cart moved spontaneously to the section of Chinese veggies.

Two hours later when my children arrived home from school, I was elbow-deep in chopping, oil was popping, music was playing, and I was deeply engaged in the art of having fun. Even now, thinking of that long-ago afternoon fills me with such a quiet sense of contentment. Pulling the thread of fun had released me from the brooding heaviness of my worries. It had reminded me of the smooth purity of riding a wave of momentary grace. And, you know what? My friend Deb was right. Returning to that space allowed me to open the cavernous expansion of my truest self in a way that organically began the flow of all the solutions I had been seeking in the first place.

Life is as we want it—either suffering or joy. If we assist in the growth of the negative, suffering results; if we help the positive forces to increase, we share in the joy of life. I think you might like the following quote from the writer Katerina Stoykova: "There is no beauty in sadness. No honor in suffering. No growth in fear. No relief in hate. It's just a waste of perfectly good happiness."[5] Your approach to life seems to echo this sentiment in a real, action-oriented way. You must be an incredible support to your extended family—your fierce commitment to feeling your own internal happiness is a motivating force in the healing process.

I think your comments regarding the energetic connection between people and events is interesting. I understand how your memory of the evening prior to this discovery would be colored with anxiety, potentially making you feel unsettled or even suspect of feelings of intuition. Using your intuition can be so profoundly helpful in so many ways—particularly for someone who hopes to work in a creative capacity. I happen to believe that life is filled with abstractions—good, bad, scary, exciting, beautiful, etc. The only way to make sense of it all is through our intuition. Intuition is seeing the solution—seeing it and knowing it. It's emotion and intellect going together. It is the most essential quality in the

---

5. Katerina Stoykova, *Bird on a Window Sill* (Lexington, KY: Accents Publishing, 2018), 20.

expansion of one's personal creativity. I encourage you to tap into that intuitive self as often as possible—I assure you, there is far more beauty there than fear.

I am excited to watch from the sidelines as your life unfolds. I have a feeling you have much to offer the world—your quiet dignity, strength, and kind understanding is infectious. You have developed a rare kind of compassion—one that comes from knowing, at the visceral level, what constitutes real pain. The beauty of this truth, however, is that you do not sit in that pain or judge others from a warped perspective that colors your understanding. Rather, you look at life with a reverence that is inspiring.

Thank you for sharing your story with such openness. Knowing your story will make me a better teacher by helping to expand my own compassion for others. Witnessing your grace, sense of humor, and dignity over the course of the semester was a source of great joy and inspiration for me.

Love,

Molly

Ninth Week

What Roles Do You Play?

Approved attributes and their relation to face make every man his
own jailer; this is a fundamental social constraint even though each
man may like his cell.

—Erving Goffman

We're Off to See the . . . Scarecrow?

One of my favorite—and most successful—thought experiments in class is
my "casting" of *The Wizard of Oz*. Walking into class with a high degree
of enthusiasm, I immediately suggest we pretend we are a summer stock
theater company. I assign roles for *The Wizard of Oz*—always placing my
student "least likely to play a dog" on stage as Toto. This is a midsemester
game, so we've typically established a friendly rapport in class. There are
always laughs as I insist that my Oz pound on his desk proclaiming, "I am
the great and mighty Oz!" or as Glinda is asked to wave her fairy wand
while addressing Dorothy in a sweet, glittery, sing-song voice.

Of course, there are only about eight "good" parts in *The Wizard of
Oz*, so the bulk of the class is assigned the role of "extras." Sweeping my
arm dramatically across the classroom, I say, "Everyone on the left side of
the room gets to be—a munchkin! The right side—a flying monkey! The
rest of you can be citizens of Oz." A sigh of disappointment runs through
the room as my "extras" exchange shy glances of resignation.

"What if," I ask the class, "after several summers of working together,
one of you decided you wanted to switch roles with someone else? Say,

one of my flying monkeys decided she wanted to play the part of the Scarecrow? Do you think Ben would trade parts happily?" We play out scenario after scenario, finally imagining one committed flying monkey edging out to the front of the stage to play a shadow Scarecrow despite the lack of an invitation. Of course, no one in the cast knows how to react to this rag-tag Scarecrow in their midst—the flying monkeys are out of formation, Toto nips at the pretend Scarecrow's heels, and Dorothy totally loses her cool in the ensuing confusion. Everyone agrees it's a ridiculous scene that creates panic, upset energy, and disarray. For the sake of order, we all agree, things work better when everyone knows their place on the stage.

Talk about opening a can of worms.

All the World's a Stage

Let's start with the understanding that identity remains unintelligible unless it is located in the known world. Every time my students show up in class ready to learn, they confirm to me that I am a teacher. When I go home to feed my children, I am a mom. When I am buying my groceries, I am a shopper. At the doctor's office, I am a patient. Our roles change constantly and automatically depending on social context. One of the easiest ways to conceptualize how naturally we do this is to think of a time when you accidently brought the wrong role to an interaction. For example, my children and husband will roll their eyes, toss their hands in the air, and groan mercilessly if I begin a sentence with "research confirms."

This is not to suggest that the roles we play completely recede during different interactions. Being a parent informs my teaching experience in rich ways. We are layered, multidimensional creatures wired to play numerous roles in any one life.

The sociologist Erving Goffman employed Shakespeare's famous metaphor to offer a conceptual framework for understanding the subjective experience of everyday life:

> All the world's a stage
> And all the men and women merely players.
> They have their exits and their entrances.
> And one man in his time plays many parts.[1]

---

1. William Shakespeare, *As You Like It*, act 2, scene 7.

The individual learns which qualities are desirable by participating in social life—the making and taking of roles. Goffman, an adherent of the symbolic interactionalist approach, explored how individuals define themselves through social interaction. Importantly, and by extension, he also wrote about how shared ideas regarding identity form the basic building blocks of cultural social life. In other words, human social behavior can be seen as more or less *scripted* according to the roles individuals take on during different interactions as defined by particular situations and environments.

Years ago in an Introduction to Sociology course, I asked students to go out and break a social code. Mind you, I made it clear they were to do nothing illegal or deviant—just to switch things up in an unexpected way and observe the response. Students enjoyed this assignment and got pretty creative in its implementation. One of my favorite rule-breakers was the young man who stood in the hallway just past the bathrooms. As people exited the bathrooms, he would ask if they had remembered to wash their hands. Sometimes when people would nod affirmatively, he would say, "Hmmm . . . that's funny. I didn't hear the water running!" My other favorite would have to be the young woman who rode the Detroit bus up and down Woodward all day long serving hors d'oeuvres. While she was frequently greeted with suspicion, she ended up getting one bus in full party mode—music blaring and people dancing in the aisle while munching mini spinach pies.

Our identity is the cumulative result of knowing ourselves through the roles we play and the routine interactions of everyday life. Human beings are naturally curious, reflective creatures. We learn from experience. We know who we are—in part—by recognizing what we are not. We act to meet the expectations of others, and certain expectations are built into our everyday life experience regarding what we will find in particular spaces and from particular people. For example, I wouldn't be able to run an effective classroom if my students ran around the room hitting each other while I attempted to lecture. It would also be awfully strange if your waiter sat down at your table and demanded to share your food. And we don't generally expect a stranger to hand us a stuffed mushroom cap on a bus ride into work. Certainly, there are occasions when events occur within different interactions that run counter to expectation. But, most of the time, we get what we expect.

Perhaps the most important lesson we learn in life is that people are much more complicated than we assume. We all have a bit of the Wicked Witch and the Cowardly Lion within us, even if we are trying hard to stand tall in our ruby slippers. Despite that fact, we tend to pigeonhole people into predetermined categories. We do this spontaneously and automatically in the role-taking and role-making of our everyday life. And this is why we often end up playing the role of flying monkey one or two seasons too long. In order to shake up stale casting choices, we need to become aware of our underlying beliefs and biases. We need to develop self-awareness so that we are able to actively choose our responses rather than simply follow old and potentially inaccurate scripts of behaviors.

Peeling back the layers of self doesn't happen overnight. Our identities exist as the result of billions of interactions and cumulative layers of experience. We confirm to ourselves over and over again what it is we believe to be true about ourselves and others. These beliefs get in the way of our ability to see beneath the surface level of ourselves and others. Importantly, they keep us from truly connecting with others in a meaningful way.

On the day of President Barack Obama's first inauguration, I wanted to do something special. I had spent the year volunteering for his campaign and had a few invitations to revel in "our" success with my fellow suburban volunteers. I had noticed on the Obama campaign site that they were calling for Inauguration Day to be a day of service. The site listed local shelters, soup kitchens, and social service centers as places to bring donations or make financial donations. While I perused the site, I stumbled on one listing that piqued my interest: a Baptist church in Detroit hosting a celebratory community luncheon.

The day of the inauguration, I went to the best bakery in town and purchased a few dozen gorgeous frosted sugar cookies. At the last minute, I decided to pull my two girls out of school to accompany me. The whole drive downtown, they peppered me with questions and whined about missing gym class.

The luncheon was in the basement of an East Side Detroit church. When we entered, both girls got shy quickly. They were right: we didn't know anyone there. We were also the only white people there—a new experience for my girls. For many white people, being the minority in a crowd is an unfamiliar (and sometimes unsettling) experience. This type of role reversal, especially for members of a privileged majority, offers the chance to grow our understanding of the role we occupy in the larger society, and what it might be like to be haphazardly cast in a different role that does not come with the same privilege. Stepping into an unfamiliar role on an unfamiliar set can also be fraught—will we be seen as frauds, booed off the stage?—but it can provide the opportunity to act authentically, because we must act without a script. And when our words and actions come from a place of authenticity, real connection with others becomes possible.

An older man in a sport coat greeted us at the door: "May I help you?"

I specifically remember feeling so shy and almost embarrassed by my potential intrusiveness. I handed him the cookies and said, "We're just so happy about President Obama's victory. We wanted to share the day with others we guessed might feel the same."

At that, he silently pulled me into a huge bear hug and invited us to stay for the celebration.

The church was decorated with balloons and streamers, and a large, big-screen TV hung precariously from a beam. There was a lovely buffet set up, where my cookies were a welcome but unneeded surprise. There wasn't a dry eye in the room as Obama was sworn in to office. We wept in our shared relief, our joy, and our inspired hopefulness for a brighter future. One older woman I talked to during lunch cried while she told me about the first time she was able to vote.

That day offered me a great gift. I recognized with some immediacy that I could not grasp the depth of feeling that Obama's victory elicited in the Black community. That doesn't mean that my own joy was insincere or meaningless, just that the full narrative of how we arrived at that day differed. The varying journeys we took to get to that church basement matter. There are a lot of ways we can put ourselves in someone else's shoes, but there are some roles we'll never know what it's like to play. Being aware of that fact is important, too.

Growing awareness helps us to move from separation to one reality. As long as you follow a script, unquestionably play a role, or maintain inflexible ideas about the individuals you meet, you will continually get what you expect. Or worse yet, what you have been told to expect. You will remain limited in your understanding of the nature of the world. Becoming aware of the roles we play and why we play them is the first step to growing the awareness that is needed to actualize our best selves.

Getting Off My Notes

My first teaching assignment at CCS was a required humanities course. I was issued a mandated textbook that outlined in some detail every important cultural and historical event of the twentieth century. Oh, the

responsibility! Each week I would set myself up at my kitchen table surrounded by books, notes, pens, and paper. Scribbling furiously, committed
to covering everything, I was intent on ensuring that I transmitted all the
important facts to my young charges.

Armed with papers, stockpiled with notes and slides, I would arrive
in class each week ready to lecture. Typically, I would start class with a
line like this: "Karl Marx's eight hundred pages of *Das Kapital* are, in a
sense, quite Hegelian." Honestly, I am blushing with embarrassment as I
recount this unfortunate story.

One day, well into the semester, I looked up and noticed that many
of my students had fallen asleep. Not the head-bobbing, trying-to-stay-
awake type of dozing, but the head-back, drooling kind of sincere sleep.
Rather than feel the shame of the situation, I laughed and said, "I'm not
very good, am I?" They smiled, and together we laughed at the ridicu-
lousness of the situation.

In his book *The Presentation of Self in Everyday Life*, Erving Goffman
writes about the impact of face-to-face interaction on identity development.[2]
Goffman's work was the first to establish the validity of researching human
behavior in social situations. It was Goffman who originally wrote about the
"belief" in the part that one is playing as the strongest aspect of identity
development. In other words, our own commitment to our "perceived"
character is the result of our own total immersion in the part that we are
playing at any given moment. Goffman writes, "And to the degree that
the individual maintains a show before others that he himself does not
believe, he can come to experience a special kind of alienation from self
and a special kind of wariness of others."[3] Oh, Erving, the shame of it all!

And what, you may be asking yourself, does this "Goffman" inter-
lude have to do with "getting off my notes?" Truth is, my failure that
first semester came as a result of my dedication to *playing out the role
of teacher*. As Goffman suggests, I was guilty of putting on a show! The
implications of this reality are profound. You see, I was so taken by the
responsibility of being a good teacher that I had forgotten to bring my
whole self to the act of teaching. My concentration on performing the
role of teacher led to a narrowness of interaction, an inability to connect
with my students, and a deep-seated insecurity. As Goffman suggests,

---

2. Erving Goffman, *The Presentation of Self in Everyday Life* (New York: Anchor, 1959).

3. Goffman, *Presentation of Self*, 57.

I became a prisoner in a cage of my own making. I was so taken with my own performance, my notes became a necessary prop to ensure my professionalism, identity, and confidence.

Getting off my notes has been a scary process. While my attachment to them hindered my development as a teacher, releasing them required that I learn to teach in the moment, learn how to connect with my students, and count on my ability to share what I know in an organic way.

While I am still a work in progress, I have made major strides in growing my confidence as a teacher. Less motivated by professional desires, I act as a more natural force in the classroom. Most importantly, getting off my notes released me from my commitment to role-playing. It expanded my perception of myself and reminded me that the very nature of notes is to bind the teaching experience. The freedom that comes with acting as myself rather than my role is like no other freedom I have ever known.

Student Paper: Bill—I Wanted to Be a Jedi Knight

When I was a kid, all I wanted was to be a Jedi Knight.

I lived and breathed everything that had to do with *Star Wars*. Watching characters like Luke Skywalker and Obi-Wan Kenobi on the TV screen in my parents' basement, while my brother and I would reenact scenes from the films with our own lightsabers and blasters, was just about the most average day of my childhood. I would even go so far as to say that those were some of my fondest childhood memories. We both were inspired by the heroism of Luke Skywalker and his group of equally heroic rebel friends. Seeing them take on the evil empire and taking part in insanely epic lightsaber duels was the coolest thing in the world for us. We owned all the movies, had an enormous collection of action figures and spaceships, and of course we had our own lightsabers that saw action just about every day.

I didn't embark on my insane obsession with *Star Wars* with just my brother, though. It was the same way with all of my elementary school pals. We would also share epic lightsaber duels and exchange lines of dialogue from the films on the playground every day. For me that was the greatest part of school as a kid. I couldn't stand listening to any of my teachers drone on and on about whatever extremely boring subject they wanted us to know about. I was literally restless to get outside. I would be the kid who was whispering to all of his pals during a lecture and was repeatedly asked to stop talking throughout the class. I was sent out into the hall if that wasn't possible. And about halfway into the day, we would get our lunch and recess, where school seemed to make perfect sense for a bit. Where I could be the kid I wanted to be, and do what I wanted to do for a while. I had a best friend, Anthony, during those years between first and fifth grade. He was just as much of a nut about this stuff as I was, and was just as uncooperative with the education system as I was. During those years a lot of friends in the group swapped in and out, as it naturally sort of happens around those ages, but he was always there at my side. He was the textbook definition of a best friend for a long time.

As the years went on and we both entered our first year of middle school, the dynamic changed. These were the start of the years where everyone started to become more aware of their place in the social structure of our middle school. Everyone started to care about how they were perceived by other kids. Anthony started playing football that summer before we started middle school. Personally I couldn't have given a damn about the other kids at that point in time; I was the same Jedi Knight in the making that I was a few years back, maybe just a bit more mature. My mentality remained the same: the things that I cared about and was interested in took priority over everything and everyone else. Over that summer upon entering middle school, Anthony became good friends with his new teammates, who incidentally were the cool kids that everyone aspired to be. During those few summer months I barely heard anything from him, and barely saw him at all. I knew he was playing sports and that took up most of his time, and thought nothing of it. I had no idea of what the social ramifications of that meant when we got back to school.

But when we did return to school, I found out quickly how one summer can wreak havoc on one's life. Basically, I was out. Anthony pretended not to know me or pay any attention to me, and just hung out with his new, much more socially superior friends. And I hated all of them for it. I hated Anthony too. I was spiteful. I hated that I lost my friend who I thought the world of and I hated that I got left at the door with nothing for not being cool enough. When it came down to it, being a part of the popular and socially superior group seemed more important to him than whatever we had. We stopped talking and hanging out, and our families have seen little of each other since.

Being left behind for "better friends" made me feel a lot of self-doubt and insecurity about myself over the next few years. I felt like I was on the outside looking in. I didn't get along with most people. Looking back now, after thinking about some of the topics that we have discussed in this class, I think that this event in my life was huge for my sense of identity in school. After feeling abandoned by and inadequate to my friend, I felt "lesser than" the cool kids. This made me seclude myself and become less social over the next few years, further changing the landscape of my social life.

Which brings me to the first time I ever fell in love with somebody. I consider myself a novice to this aspect of life, and at the time this story took place, I had never truly fallen in love with another person before. But I met a girl in one of my classes in college, and from the first time that I saw her, I knew she was different. I had barely exchanged five words with her in my whole life, but I just got a feeling from her that I had never felt before and couldn't even explain. In the months that we had this class together I inched my way closer and closer to her, each time more nervous than the last. I just had to get a chance to make something happen with her.

I finally asked her out on a date after a few weeks . . . and she said yes. I was thrilled and felt on top of the world for a bit. We went out about a week later for coffee, and after spending only about three hours with her, I was floored. She was educated, interesting, polite, funny, and stunningly beautiful. It seemed too good to be true that she would waste her time on a schmuck like me! I felt so inferior to her in every aspect. And as it turned out, it *was* too good to be true. She wasn't fully aware that I intended this as a date, and told me afterward that she wasn't looking to see anybody at that time. It made me upset that she wasn't interested, especially since we hit it off so well and I was so into her.

Still, I was determined to win her over. I spent the next few months hanging out with her, getting to know her well, being as much of a gentleman as I could, doing nice things for her, and trying to make her see my worth. Over these months, I was riding a rollercoaster of emotions. This was also at a time when I'd had a change of heart in terms of my career path, and was feeling that my dozen years of schooling and my ambition to this point had been misguided—even wasted. As I struggled to find my footing, and as I struggled with my schoolwork, none of those things even came close to the anxiety I felt about her. She was always on my mind. As all these months passed, I grew crazier and crazier about her, and I stepped up my game to maximum.

One night before the next semester started, we were together and I couldn't be patient any longer with her. I just wanted to do what I thought was right, and I tried to kiss her. She stopped me, and told me she couldn't do this with me. The way she told me and the way she looked at me, I knew it was the truth—how she really felt. I let her go, and I tried to move on.

For months to follow, I was depressed. I drank pretty heavily and got the heaviest into smoking that I ever had; I felt like everything came crashing down. I lost track of my career goals, my schooling was falling down a bit, and I felt that the one person that I'd ever felt a true connection with I couldn't have, no matter how hard I tried. It was the absolute worst I'd ever felt about myself. I felt inadequate, stupid, and defeated on every front.

This was such an important moment. Before, I'd never known the true impact of connecting with another person, regardless of whether or not the feeling was one-sided. I hadn't considered how important this was to the development of the self. I'd always looked inward to find meaning in my life; this experience marked the first time that meaning was about *more* than just myself. When we had been together, I'd felt the most fulfilled in my life. There were times when I got to hold her and just be with her; in those moments, I felt like the best version of myself that had ever existed.

At the same time, the experience of falling in love with her also offered times that made me feel my lowest lows, my biggest defeats. The effect this had on me mentally was excruciating. I think looking back and understanding it for what it was has made me a stronger man, and maybe—hopefully—more prepared for the next time it happens. At the end of this life experience, I can definitely say it had a profound effect on the way that I saw myself and the world around me.

There are moments in not only my life, but in all of our lives, that make us question how and why we have gotten to a certain place and time. They make us question how much impact specific moments we've experienced have had on us. Looking back, there have been many big moments in my life that have changed the way I view the world and how I am a part of it. But there have also been just as many smaller moments in my life that have had the same impact on my way of thinking and my overall decision-making process. Some of these moments are the result of choice, some of chance, and some of uncertainty.

The knowledge I've gained from this class on identity, the chance to practice meditation, and the research I've done on the writings and research of Harry L. Gracey, Raymond Williams, and Neil Postman have helped me to analyze the personally impactful moments that have shaped my life. Feeling the wholeness of my being during meditation has helped me to look objectively at these moments as abstracted images meant to offer new insights into who I am and who I hope to become. Hopefully, through continued meditation practice, I can achieve an understanding of how to continue to organically grow my consciousness and develop a keen sociological imagination on a daily basis.

Dear Bill—

There is so much to enjoy about your paper, but mostly I am just in love with your honesty. It has always been my opinion that we create our own story line every day through the choices that we make. Our internal landscape is informed by our daily interactions: feeling building upon feeling. Over time our notions about ourselves are pretty well defined, and our behavior becomes an almost automatic process of confirming what it is we believe to be true about ourselves. Patterns that are set in childhood are typically hard to break. I admire your willingness to work to change your perspective.

I just hate the story about how your friendship with Anthony ended. And, while I have read countless other versions of the same story, they always hurt my heart. Wounded feelings at a vulnerable age can really shape your confidence. Feeling left out and isolated is a terrible feeling. I also happen to think it is a universal feeling. Ironically, it is often felt the most acutely by those who desire connectivity the most.

One of the greatest pieces of wisdom my mother ever shared with me was the following: "We only see in others what we hold within ourselves." The reason I love this wisdom is that it helps me to connect rather than to distance from those around me. It reminds me to see things through a prism of wholeness rather than separateness, and ultimately it helps me to feel more connected to everything and everyone around me. In this case, it also offers you the quiet awareness that if you can "see" the cool factor, you also have that internal ability to play that card, too.

Your reflections on love also struck a chord with me. Love is born out of allurement—a gravitational pull toward something. This allurement or attraction is related to good smells, a soft touch, a pleasing image, a shared laugh. Love is born out of this attraction. With meditation and the expansion of consciousness, a new form of love spontaneously flows through us. This love is a love for the sake of love. A love related less to a figure-it-out mentality of evaluation but the simple flow of love as an undercurrent of feeling. An internal lighting up in the mere presence of another.

Sometimes I think we confuse feelings of "desire" for "love." And feelings of love can sometimes seamlessly merge with feelings of desire. Culturally, this connection is continuously reinforced by the media, by conversation, by our understanding of modes of expression. But in truth, love and desire are distinct from one another. Certainly, expressing our love in a physical way can be meaningful and enjoyable. But it is not necessarily a required parallel action to be pursued every time we feel the stirrings of love deep in our heart. This is not a judgment. It is simply a reflection that I think is often overlooked in our hypersexualized culture. More importantly, a heart capable of feeling love with such immediacy should be cherished and nurtured. It is a brave and noble heart.

The end of your paper shows such a quiet dignity. I think the hardest thing anyone ever does is truly look in the mirror and shift those patterns that they know are no longer working. It requires great patience and forgiveness. I love the stories you chose to share with me. They are some of the most honest, dignified truths a student has ever offered me. Perhaps your biggest hurdle is to just forgive your sweet self for taking the time to grow up (oh, what a luxury in our fast-paced, crazed world!). Taking your time to find what you "like" to do, who you want to love, and how to be a friend seem like pretty darn good lessons to me.

Your paper is basically there. You did a great job; a quick edit to break up some of your long paragraphs would be helpful.

It's been a pleasure to get to know you this semester, Bill. Hope you stay in touch. I have a good feeling about the future stories you will be able to share with me.

Love,

Molly

Tenth Week

How Do Labels Define Us—and Confine Us?

I want to make people understand that boxing ourselves into tiny cubbies based on class, race, ethnicity, religion—anything, really—comes from a poverty of mind, a poverty of imagination. The world is dull and cruel when we isolate ourselves.

—Clemantine Wamariya and Elizabeth Weil

Pepe le Chat

A favorite little metaphor of mine is the black cat who accidently gets white paint smeared down his back. Now, as he innocently wanders the neighborhood, people mistake him for a skunk. Poor little black cat no longer finds kibbles and bits left at the back door of grandma's house. As he approaches children playing on the street, they drop their bats and balls in horror. That cat now has a stigma or a label attached to him. No one wants to play with Pepe le Chat!

Craft Arts Majors Are Potheads

During introductions on the first day of class, I always ask students why they have chosen to sign up. Given the unique nature of the course, pretty much everyone has a reason. For most, the answer is that they look forward to learning to meditate. Many tell me that a friend recommended they register. My favorite response is "it just fit the time slot." (That student becomes tagged as "So-and-so of low expectations"—they are generally the easiest to please!). More and more often, though, students say to me, "I heard about your 'label' lecture."

Ah, the label lecture: tricky, tricky work. For years in my Intro to Sociology courses, race, class, and gender were discussed as primary topics. I employed a number of different exercises recommended in books to dispel stereotypes, illuminate the value of diversity, and expose the role of bias and injustice in our culture. We tossed grenades back and forth in an effort to expose stereotypes and labels. Everyone was offered a chance to speak, share perspectives, and explore the meaning behind cultural differences. The goal of these discussions was to support students' identities and to create a classroom environment where individuals could be their most authentic selves. Additionally, these conversations were motivated by my desire to bridge the divide between different groups and build genuine value for diversity. And, at times, I felt these conversation did just that—our discussions offered students an effective way to connect ideas learned in school and in practical life settings. But sometimes, and then later most of the time, I felt these discussions simply exacerbated our divides, put people in defensive territory, or, worse yet, created an atmosphere where all my students insisted that "old" people (namely, me) didn't understand the "color-blind" culture that the YouTube/social media world had created (according to them). Thus, the birth of the "label" lecture.

CCS is an art and design school made up of about fifteen departments. My department, liberal arts, is the one department that captures everyone. The different departments each have unique qualities and cater to diverse students. The competitive energy between departments is occasionally intense. I think it is safe to say that pretty much everyone feels that their department is misunderstood and undervalued in comparison to other departments. Most students view other departments and often, by extension, individual students, through the lens of these feelings of victimization and insecurity. Using this cultural template as a backdrop becomes a pretty good way to explore how labels and stereotypes limit our understanding of "others."

The label lecture begins with me asking the students to sit with others from their department. The first twenty minutes of our time together is devoted to exploring all the stereotypes they have ever heard about their department. I tell them not to hold back; the goal of this exercise is to pull out all the rumors, misinformation, and truths about your department.

The second part of this exercise is to make a list of stereotypes about other majors. Trust me when I tell you my class explodes into giddy excitement and laughter. They are literally gleeful with this opportunity to deconstruct, pick apart, and share their observations about the CCS culture.

I start the conversation the same way every semester: "What do you guys think, should we let the photo kids go first? Let's get them out of the way. I mean, is photography really even art? Can't anyone take a picture these days?" The room explodes. And, so it begins.

Truly, once you disarm the conversation, the juices start to flow. The photo kids admit to being basement dwellers. They acknowledge that many of them found photography during their angst-filled teenage years. They laugh hysterically when they realize they all have on black from head to toe and sport at least three tattoos. After they finish their own list, I ask the class if they've missed anything. Someone typically yells, "They all hang outside the photo lab smoking Camels twenty-four-seven!" And, the photo kids nod and agree, "Oh, yeah, we forgot that—guess we're in denial."

Then, I say, "So, photo kids, what do you want other people on campus to know about your major?" Immediately, my photo kids sit up taller in their seats, simultaneously proclaiming, "It's hard to take a picture! Our equipment is super expensive and changing all the time. We continuously have to update our equipment and relearn the technology. Lighting is a tremendously nuanced process. . . ." It goes on and on.

We have a ball during "label lecture" week. It's a hilarious, humbling, revealing, and empowering conversation. My animators admit to being "furries," the graphic design kids acknowledge that Comic Sans gives them a headache, and the crafters come clean about having smoked "just one joint" before class. We look around the room and acknowledge that all the interior design students are women. And the transportation designers are Asian. There are, of course, always exceptions to the "rules," but we collectively acknowledge that stereotypes hold weight because there is often a grain of truth to them.

To me, the most interesting part of the class session comes near the end. It is when the class slowly begins to recognize two things: (1) Every department is intricately connected to every other department. (2) There are intrinsic burdens as well as unique opportunities available to students of every major. Ironically, a large part of this recognition comes in the acknowledgment that no department is more utilized as a collaborator than photography. In the end, we come full circle. Turns out, despite their "prejudice," many students are dependent on the skills of a professional photographer when they need to showcase their work.

There are many other nuanced realizations that come to light during this exercise. Most are particular to CCS and less relevant to this book, but I imagine you understand the contribution this exercise makes to teaching critical engagement. Teaching students to recognize the truth embedded in our own words is as important as teaching students how to listen and how to hear one another. Creating an environment in the classroom where students learn to both speak and listen can be challenging. There must be a balance between constructive critique of ideas and the real understanding of the legitimacy of different perspectives.

In its Declaration of Principles on Tolerance, UNESCO offers the following definition: "Tolerance is harmony in difference."[1] In other words, the pathway to tolerance moves straight through the recognition of difference. Martin Luther King used the Greek term "agape" to describe the ideal of a universal love for every person, regardless of race, religious, or political beliefs. This type of philosophical love serves as the emotional undercurrent for true tolerance. Running headlong into this profound truth, however, creates an awkward moment where we sit in agreement with no place to go. In reality, conversations about tolerance require students to be both critical and respectful at the same time. This is a tough space to navigate. Coming at it sideways—via the CCS label exercise—creates the space to explore some uncomfortable truths about our assumptions and biases about others. It provides more than a few "aha" moments of recognition and builds tolerance for others in a richly organic way. It allows us to talk about labels without getting defensive, and to ask some pertinent questions:

On any given day, how often do we unconsciously label other individuals? What are the labels that others might apply to us? Do these labels describe every aspect of our identities? Which labels are we eager to claim and which labels are we quick to reject? How do we feel when we are labeled by others? Why do we use labels in the first place?

The fact is, we understand the world via contrast—hot versus cold, win versus lose, on versus off, and so on. In sociology, we refer to this

---

1. UNESCO Office of International Standards and Legal Affairs, "Declaration of Principles on Tolerance," UNESCO website, November 1995, http://portal.unesco. org/en/ev.php-URL_ID=13175&URL_DO=DO_TOPIC&URL_SECTION=201.html.

concept as binary opposition—pairs of opposites that are defined by contrast with each other. We encounter binary oppositions in the study of culture when we explore relationships between different groups of people, for example upper class and lower class, or disabled and able-bodied. This way of understanding the world leads to labeling people and things by describing what they are in contrast with what they are not.

The problem with gaining knowledge of something by comparing it with its opposite is that we tend to judge one side of the pair as positive and one as negative—another binary opposition! Making sense of the world by comparing and contrasting people, experiences, and objects is part of the human experience. That said, the process often obscures the complexity of our lives. Labels do not capture the essence of understanding or the fullness of experience and identities for individual people.

Labeling a person can have positive results. For example, when schools apply for federal funding for special services for students with disabilities, they may be required to label students in order to receive money or provide appropriate accommodations. While labels—particularly in medical or educational settings—are often useful in communication with other professionals in order to determine special services, they rarely tell us much about a person. In fact, it is often noted that labels cause individuals stigma, resulting in isolation and loneliness.[2]

A person's self-image is tied to the words used to describe that person. The language we use when speaking of other people sets a tone. It shows how we perceive them and their worth. Our word choices reflect our beliefs and our biases. It is easy to overgeneralize our knowledge of and experiences with others without really getting to know individual people.

In my experience, the scariest thing about the way we toss labels and stereotypes around is the way we pretend they are not humanly created and perpetuated. We assume a one-size-fits-all mentality when we label others, ignoring the possibility that the label only describes one tiny aspect of the person we seek to define. We ignore the full range of an individual's potential, their inner life, and the richness of their experiences. We cut people down, reducing them to fragmented aspects of themselves. While a label may capture a momentary expression of an individual, it does not tell a complete story.

---

2. Joan Susman, "Disability, Stigma Deviance," *Social Science & Medicine* 38, no. 1 (January 1994): 15–22, doi: https://doi.org/10.1016/0277^p 536(94)90295-X.

The Mother of a Disabled Child

Some years after my son Charlie's recovery, a friend called asking what words of advice I might offer to a colleague with a child in a similar state of indefinable illness. Knowing that there were no "right" words to offer, I sat for a long time staring at my computer.

Dear Susan—

It is important that you know the end of my story before you hear the beginning. I have a perfectly healthy, strong, and wonderful ten-year-old son who started life in much the same condition as your daughter. He is not on a special diet. He does not take any medication. He has not seen a medical specialist in over seven years.

Like you, my husband and I were desperate for a diagnosis for our son. But, I must warn you, as one very courageous doctor warned me: be mindful of what you wish for. The medical community will be desperate to diagnose your daughter—that is what they do—but you must remember in defining disease they also create the environment for the disease to sustain itself. While you may have to struggle through this time, your goal is to have your baby "grow out" of this illness. You must allow for her body to repair itself. It is possible.

Love,

Molly

What I did not share with Susan was the following: a few weeks after Charlie was born, still not knowing what was wrong with him or whether he would recover, I heard a terrible noise. It was guttural in nature—a low, deep-throated noise—followed by bursts of laughing and children yelling. For the life of me, I could not figure out where it came from. Eventually, I realized that there was a disabled child playing in the yard attached to ours. In his joyous excitement, he was making this terrible noise. My reaction: to fly through the house, weeping and slamming the windows shut. I still feel shame when I think of that hot afternoon. But that child scared me. He represented a potential future that I was determined to steadfastly deny: a future in which I would be "the mother of a disabled child."

In that moment, I felt the fear of a label being applied to my son that would affect how the world saw him, and, by extension, our whole family. How would it affect Charlie's identity to be labeled as "disabled" or otherwise different from other children? How would it feel to know that people saw me as "the mom of that handicapped boy" rather than "the mom of those three adorable kids"? And, as I intimated to Susan in my letter, would rushing to apply a potentially inaccurate diagnosis to my baby actually perpetuate his illness?

When I reflect on Charlie's illness, I find myself most grateful to the courageous Dr. Souheil Gebara. It was he who suggested that Charlie might just have an immature organ system. He looked at me so kindly and said, "You know, Mrs. Beauregard, we like to pretend that we are Gods who can cure all ailments. But, in reality, we understand so little about the way the human body functions. Sometimes it is the little ones who surprise us the most with their profound resiliency." His admission of the limitations of his knowledge and his willingness to not label Charlie and his condition without sufficient knowledge offered me permission to relax into the mystery of my own son's slow beginnings.

Imagine if Charlie's doctor had not given me permission to stay in the space of the unknown. Would my determination to find a diagnosis have influenced my willingness to submit our infant to unnecessary testing? Would the risks associated with the testing have caused more harm than good, making a provisionally applied label a self-fulfilling prophecy? Thankfully, we will never know the answers to these questions.

Student Paper: Ethan—A Life Worth Acceptance

For most of history, to be gay in America automatically meant to be an outcast, someone shunned from society for the differentiation that others saw in them. We now find ourselves in a society of growing acceptance for homosexuals, as the tolerance for discrimination crumbles, and more rights are allotted to them. I, myself, am gay, and I find myself more and more thankful to be a gay man in today's society as opposed to having lived as such in a previous generational period. It took a long time to reach the point I am at in life, especially with my homosexuality. The process of going through high school hiding my sexuality, personally coming to terms with my sexuality, and lastly making my sexuality known to the world was a complex collection of events that ultimately led me to a much deeper understanding of myself beyond just my sexual orientation. I am a homosexual individual, yet homosexuality is not the means by which I define myself; however, it is the vehicle with which I am able to access a deeper understanding as to who I am both personally and within society.

I started dance when I was six years old, and as one can imagine, there was quite a bit of ridicule and teasing that I faced as I progressed through my years in school. The main focus of my teasing was the fact that being a male participating in a female sport made me gay. The teasing and the bullying, along with negative social stigmas about homosexuality that I was raised with, did not paint a very nice image of what it meant to be gay for me. That is not to say that I was raised to hate homosexuals, only that their acknowledgment was always met with a negative stigma in my family. One of the first things I always seem to be asked when someone finds out that I am gay is, "Now how long did you actually know you were gay?" to which I truthfully respond as to always possessing a sense of who I truly was in my sexual orientation.

My reason for having avoided coming out sooner can be attributed to the negative stigma that had been engrained into my head involving homosexuality. I lived in fear of the fact that I could possibly be that which was always cast in a shadow. I was never fully accepting of the fact, as I constantly made excuses or deflected my thoughts to falsely misinterpret my interest in boys as it became more and more apparent. Thoughts like, "Maybe I'm not straight, but I'm definitely not gay, so I must be bisexual" or "You're not completely checking that guy out if the girl he is with is attractive too" constantly ran through my head just to avoid accepting the fact that I was gay. Goffman eloquently explains the negative social biases I experienced in association with my dancing:

> If unacquainted with the individual, observers can glean clues from his conduct and appearance which allow them to apply their previous experience with individuals roughly similar to the one before them or, more important, to apply untested stereotypes on him. They can also assume from past experience that only individuals of a particular kind are likely to be found in a given social setting.[3]

---

3. Erving Goffman, *The Presentation of Self in Everyday Life* (New York: Doubleday, 1959), 136.

These assumptions made about me only drove me to prove them wrong. Who am I to be told who I am, based off of someone's uneducated opinion about myself? I can be a male dancer and not be gay, I can be the one to break the stereotypical mold. At this point I became extremely introverted, someone for a friend to lean on but never one to do the leaning. I feared that if I were to begin opening up, I would run the risk of someone finding out the truth about me, forcing me to face the fact that I might just be another stereotype. As predicted by my young self, nearly this exact sequence of events proved to be the downfall of my secret.

As I progressed through my adolescent and teen years I was able to develop an act that became second nature, and the more I was able to convince myself, the easier it was to convince everyone else. This act evolved to hide more than just my sexuality. I began to use it to hide my innermost feelings from myself, bottling everything away so as not to have to deal with any of it. As one can imagine, relationships with others, whether they were romantic or friendly, became difficult. To many I lacked a depth to the understanding of my feelings, never fully engaging as to how I felt to successfully keep people only as close to me as I felt comfortable.

College came to be, and I began the journey of discovering who I might be, or who I thought I wanted to be at the time, never fully accepting the ends by which I found myself, for I knew deep down that they were all a lie, that something was missing. By my sophomore year, I finally reached the point in understanding that the negative stigmas I grew to know did not actually apply to me. It was not wrong for me to be gay, and if I wanted to understand myself, I had to first accept myself. The acceptance did not wash over me in one solid wave of understanding, but as a slow drip as the permafrost of my past being slowly began to warm. As I grew into myself, I began talking to boys on a more romantic level, testing the waters of my sexuality to get a feel as to what it was that I had been denying myself for so many years. On this journey of acceptance, barriers started to break down, and I began losing track of how close I allowed people to get. My closest friend at the time had had a strong dislike for a boy I decided to go to lunch with, and knowing of her distaste for him, I unsuccessfully attempted to hide it from her. Obviously, she found out, and was rightfully hurt when she confronted me for an explanation. This friend was one of the individuals who I had allowed to get close recently, and she did not accept my default reaction of silence and declination. She pushed for answers as to my recent change in character and my having lied to her, which I held off until I ultimately snapped. The dam broke and my pulse quickened as I finally released with a gasp my longest held secret. "I think I'm gay . . ." was the only response I could muster in response to her barrage of questions. At that point, I felt myself come full circle. C. Wright Mills best describes this struggle of self-introspection that I found myself trapped in:

> Nowadays, men often feel that their private lives are a series of traps. They sense that, within their everyday worlds, they cannot overcome their troubles, and, in this feeling, they are quite correct: What ordinary men are directly aware of and what they try to do are bounded by the private orbits in which they live; their visions and their powers are limited to the close-up scenes of job, family, neighborhood; in other milieux, they move vicariously and remain spectators.[4]

I cornered myself within my worry of my sexuality; it was the means by which I locked down all other feelings trying to protect myself from the unknown. In attempting to separate myself from the mold of homosexuality, I forced myself into another mold for which I was not meant. I then realized I did not need a mold as a definition of who I was or what I meant to myself. With this realization, I removed myself from the clutches of the passenger's seat and took my place at the wheel. I was brought into a new world of understanding where I was able to grasp the meaning behind all my emotions. If I could not comprehend a specific feeling at the time, I began to develop an ability to break it down in an attempt to gain a better understanding.

This brings us to the portion of my life where my personal development is growing exponentially. I am able to evaluate the relationships in my life and recognize those that are toxic, and those that are healthy and beneficial. I found myself in a cleansing process, ridding my life of any toxic aspects that were previously holding me back, which ultimately ushered in the end of the friendship with the person who first led me to confronting my secrets. The most important relationship that needed to be confronted was my parents. My parents are a special kind of people, in the fact that they do not show their emotions in a typical fashion. My brothers and I know that our parents love us, yet I cannot remember

---

4. C. Wright Mills, *The Sociological Imagination* (London: Oxford University Press, 1959), 20.

the last time I received or gave either of my parents a hug. They show their affection and caring through different aspects, aspects that would be undetectable to anyone not surrounded in their environment for twenty years. The task of coming out to your parents, especially ones as conservative as mine, is a daunting one, and was one that I knew could not be tackled all at once. I would have to divide them up to lessen the impact that they would feel. The act I utilized to hide myself from the world came with such ease because of my past familiarity with it. It was a trait I learned from my mother, an individual who is the most private and hidden person I have yet to meet.

I have a deeper connection than most with my mother, based on an understanding as to how and why she operates the way she does. She was be the one I came out to first because I knew she would be the one to take it the hardest. Her world would be altered the most drastically. I did not beat around the bush, and told her up front that I was gay. I tried to my best ability to break down my journey of acceptance in a way that she would be able to understand. Her confusion was clear, and her response, expected. "How do you know? You might be able to accept it that easily, but I can't, it's not natural. . . ." A sense of betrayal was palpable. I was her golden child, the oldest and most successful to date. I was the child that was to be the pinnacle of her success as a parent, and she saw my sexuality as a stain of that reflection of herself. She did not have to explain any of this to me, I just knew; I understood because the stance was similar to my original attitude to my sexuality before my awakening. After that, there was a solid three months of silence between the two of us. A silence that was not welcome or comfortable on my part, but a silence that was necessary for her as she embarked on the same journey of acceptance I had only months earlier.

Knowing her struggle and the fact that she would try to hide it from my family, I then came out to my father. His acceptance, although tentative, was enhanced by his ultimate love for his son. He was now able to focus on his wife, for he immediately knew, as I knew, the struggle she faced. Robert Bellah describes this certain connection I have with my parents: "Social ecology. . . . Human beings and their societies are deeply interrelated, and the actions we take have enormous ramifications for the lives of others."[5] My father and I have come to know my mother through her

---

5. Robert N. Bellah, Richard Madsen, William M. Sullivan, Ann Swindler, and Steven M. Tipton, *Habits of the Heart: Individualism and Commitment in American Life* (Berkeley: University of California Press, 1985), 284.

attempts to keep herself closed off. She interacted and accepted people and their differences through the lens of her of own personal understanding, limited by her solitude—a struggle I knew and understood firsthand. I came to realize that this solitude was what kept me back from developing a deeper empathetic appreciation for the individuals I encountered on a day-to-day basis. Being in a similar state, this empathetic appreciation was lacking in my mother as well. Although my mother has reached a point of acceptance of me, and gets along well with my boyfriend, I do not believe she has reached this level of appreciation that I continue to develop and hone.

My journey is marked with these moments of significance that have led to who I currently am. Self-reflection brings about the realization that my traits do not fit me into any stereotypical mold. I have built a life surrounded by people whose relationships with me are based on love and our empowerment of each other. Elizabeth Lloyd Mayer views this struggle that many others find themselves facing: "We suffer from an underlying cultural disinclination for publicly acknowledging certain highly subjective, highly personal experiences. We're especially reluctant to credit those personal and subjective factors when it comes to things we prefer to be dictated by rational and objective thinking."[6] I credit the struggle I faced with my sexuality and my relationship with my mother for bringing me to this higher sense of understanding. I have no desire to connect with people based on cultural fads, and strive to understand people in their primal aspects. I am not only connected with my inner emotions, I am able to completely envelop myself in them. I am no longer afraid to feel, for I am no longer willing to limit myself to the superficial spectrum of what it means to be human. I depend on those friends and individuals I have grown close with to expand my knowledge of human interactions, a symbiotic relationship where everyone gives and takes equally in an attempt to constantly grow and expand past any trials or tribulations.

I am gay, but I do not limit myself to the cultural stereotypes that define modern homosexuality. I am a friend, and a boyfriend, but I am not an object to be abused by others for their own gain. I am my mother's son, but I do not limit myself to the emotional disconnect she finds necessary for survival in our cultural identification process. I am

6. Elizabeth Lloyd Mayer, *Extraordinary Knowing: Science, Skepticism, and the Inexplicable Powers of the Human Mind* (New York: Bantam Books, 2007), 25.

many things, but these things do not define me. I know who I was, who I am now, and who I want to be, and I am constantly learning how I can achieve the goal of constant self-improvement. My sexuality is not a means by which I define myself, it is a tool I used to connect myself to society and a vehicle by which I access a deeper understand of who I am both personally and within society.

Dear Ethan—

Thank you for writing such a beautiful, heartfelt paper. There are no rewrites necessary with this "rough," as you have understood the assignment completely. In addition to incorporating the academic readings, your willingness to place yourself squarely within the cultural context is inspiring. While acknowledging your need for continued growth, former blind spots, and pain, you peel back the layers of belief that no longer serve the Ethan you hope to become. Lastly, you do all this with grace. While focusing on your own learning, you never lose sight of how all your experiences have helped to shape who you are today.

I admire your ability to take your personal suffering and transform it into an obviously very rich and nuanced inner life. I encourage you—as you write—to continue to use your sexuality as a "tool" to connect with society and as "a vehicle by which (you) can access a deeper understanding" of yourself. It may be a defining feature of who you are, but it is not ALL that you are.

I think it is so important that people understand that identity is but one aspect of self. It is essentially the vehicle through which we make sense of the world. The purpose of growing self-awareness—and ultimately expanding consciousness—is to increase our own sense of well-being and happiness. In the deeper, more expansive reality of consciousness, you are connected to the totality of the universe. And, ultimately at your very basis, you are, simply put, a beautiful expression of the absolute nature of love. It is clear to me that you have touched this beautiful internal space. You radiate it out, Ethan, with real authentic grace.

Trust me when I tell you I have read many papers written by young people struggling with their sexuality. There is no doubt we live in a hypersexualized culture. Navigating the landscape is confusing under most circumstances. I admire your openness to explore the many nuances of your personal relationships. There is a quiet dignity seamlessly woven throughout your paper that is both compelling and inspiring.

You are a good writer—have you ever considered sharing your work publicly? I think it would resonate deeply with others facing similar growing pains. Just a thought . . .

I hope you will keep in touch. I look forward to watching your story unfold. I think you have much to look forward to. It has been a real pleasure to get to know you this semester. Thank you again for honoring me with such a lovely, honest paper.

Much love,

Molly

Eleventh Week

How Does Place Inform Our Sense of Self?

Place is attitudinal and longitudinal within the map of a person's life. It is temporal and spatial, personal and political. A layered location replete with human histories and memories, place has width as well as depth. It is about connections, what surrounds it, what formed it, what happened there, what will happen there.

—Lucy R. Lippard

Professor's Office or Prison Cell?

Picture, in your mind's eye, a small cinderblock room. The walls, dingy with dust and faded by time, are painted an institutional grey-green. A tiny window, cut high into the back wall, allows just a sliver of light to reach the surface of a steel desk. Sitting at the desk is a hunched figure wearing a nondescript outfit, a pencil tucked neatly behind their ear.

Now, feel the space. Does the scene evoke feelings of creativity, intellectualism, and concentrated effort? Or does it evoke loneliness, isolation, and searching? Or is it possible that the scene gives rise to some combination of these emotions? Perhaps this scene depicts a math professor catching up on the latest research in their field. Maybe you've imagined a bike leaning on an outside wall, a cup of coffee on the table, and a student sitting on a wooden bench just outside of view. Conversely, you may have imagined a prisoner reading just to pass time before an impending court date. In this case, a guard holding a billy club stands sternly in the hallway awaiting the transport call.

Either way, it is clear that this small room takes on completely different meanings depending on what it is used for, and by whom. Meanings, memories, and activities attached to spaces reinforce concepts of authority, autonomy, creativity, and dignity. Becoming aware of how our own activity in different spaces and on different landscapes impacts the creation of place is an important aspect of identity studies.

Layered Locations

Our concept of "place" is created through the meaning we assign a space and the activities we do there. The places where we live, work, play, and even dump waste become meaningful through our interactions with them, and in turn these places influence our identities.

Another favorite in-class exercise is to simply ask students to close their eyes and imagine their favorite place. When they have an image visualized in their mind's eye, I tell them to recount the activities they have engaged in there. The in-class conversation that typically follows becomes one of our sweetest reflections of the semester, as students share story after story of favorite ballparks, beaches, lakes, fields, and the alleyway next to grandma's house that became transformed into a magical forest during playtime with cousins after Sunday night dinner.

I'm always amazed by how many young people proclaim their basements, bedrooms, and other small, nondescript spaces as favorite spots. Once, a student silenced the room by sharing memories of her basement. She described her basement perfectly: a carpeted, 1950s-style "rec room" with a stand-up bar, natty couch, and an off-to-the-side, concrete-floored utility room housing overstuffed boxes and Tupperware bins filled with Christmas decorations and old Halloween costumes. She told the class about her middle school slumber parties, when her dad would pop his head around the corner of the stairwell to check in on her and her girl-friends. As Zoe laughingly recounted, "My dad was just so embarrassing to me. He would always toss out some goofy joke or tease us about boys or something. Even though I consistently batted him away, I secretly kinda loved it too." Zoe's dad died the summer before she came to college. She told the class, "Sometimes when I feel especially lonely for him, I visit that basement. For some reason, it is the one place I can still hear his voice, still picture his smile, and still feel his 'dad' presence as a comforting force."

Similar to my students, I have a wonderful childhood memory of an unexpected cherished spot—two long, narrow closets across from each other in the upstairs den of our Philadelphia house. It was an old house with a slanted roof, so the closets were especially quirky. My sister and I pretended that those closets were our home. The closets contained toys, books, crayons, and occasionally little treasures found outside in the backyard. My baby brother was banned from entering and could frequently be found sobbing inconsolably in a sagging diaper just outside the closet doors. My mother loves to tell the embarrassing story about a confusing moment she and my dad shared with guests who came to dinner at our house. Shortly after my sister and I, scrubbed clean and in our PJs, came downstairs to greet my parents' guests, my dad said, "Now, girls, why don't you behave yourselves and run upstairs to your closets." A good laugh was shared when it was revealed that our closets were actually little play spaces. There are few things as precious to a child as a private corner to transform into an imaginary fort, fairyland, or exotic, magical cave.

We may think that we leave behind this tendency to transform spaces using our imaginations in childhood, but as adults, we still engage in the magical creation of place, we just may not realize we're doing it. In *The Lure of the Local*, art critic Lucy Lippard writes, "Space defines landscape, where space combined with memory defines place."[1] Making a space a place requires connection, activity, and layers of interaction. When we think of landscape as holding an identity, we personalize our experiences on the land and feel responsible for our actions. Using this definition, we can understand landscape as a kind of activity, a way of seeing the world and imagining—or reimagining—our relationship to nature. What I most appreciate about this concept is that it leaves room for possibility.

Years ago, my husband and I visited Scotland. In addition to the gorgeous outdoor scenery, we scoured the country for the coziest bar in all the land. One evening, we were yukking it up with a lovely group of locals, when I happened to ask if any of them had ever seen a ghost in the old ruins just outside of town. Slapping their knees just like the old-timers of movie lore, they laughed and laughed at the backward absurdity of my assumptions. And then . . . one of the men interrupted the laughter,

---

1. Lucy Lippard, *The Lure of the Local: Senses of Place in a Multicentered Society* (New York: New Press, 1998), 9.

saying, "Well—there is Old Man Jim!" Turns out, "Old Man Jim" wanders through town each and every spring—walking directly through Mrs. Sullivan's house—wearing a suit and carrying his wicker basket, fishing rod slung over his shoulder. Mike and I laughed, exclaiming in unison, "And you accused us of being crazy!" On a more serious note, "Old Man Jim" is part of the village's landscape and its community identity. It doesn't matter if you believe the ghost is real or not; he is part of the story the locals tell about the place they conceive of as home, a story that reinforces the bonds between community members and their connection to the landscape they collectively inhabit.

The idea of ghosts and ancestors wandering the land with me as silent companions titillates my imagination. The notion that things may remain unseen, hovering just outside my own limited awareness, fills me with a sense of awe and makes every space resonate with potential and enhanced meaning. As Lippard writes, "If landscape is a way of seeing, there are potentially as many landscapes as individual ways of seeing, or at least as many as cultural ways of seeing—although some people seem threatened by this degree of multiplicity."[2] If there are endless ways of seeing any given landscape, this means that we can change the way we look at any given landscape, and thus the way we understand it. This is a powerful idea when you consider how humans have exploited and damaged the earth; the disregard we have shown for the planet and for other species comes from seeing the earth as an endless source of resources created for humans to use. If we want to change the way we treat the earth, in the hopes of preserving it for future generations of humans and other species, we must change the way we see it.

In his beautiful, evocative book *A Sacred Place to Dwell: Living with Reverence upon the Earth,* Henryk Skolimowski advocates for conceiving of the world as a sanctuary.[3] As he suggests, this habit offers "the comfort of knowing that you live in a caring, spiritual place, that the universe has meaning and your life has meaning."[4] This mind-set also elevates the human experience by connecting it to responsible living, choice-making, and visionary seeing. Living in the world with reverence requires understanding your personal connection to natural habitats. "To act in the

---

2. Lippard, *The Lure of the Local,* 61.

3. Henryk Skolimowski, *A Sacred Place to Dwell: Living with Reverence upon the Earth* (Rockport, MA: Element Books, 1993).

4. Skolimowski, *A Sacred Place to Dwell,* 6.

world as if it were a sanctuary is to make it reverential and sacred; and is to make yourself elevated and meaningful."[5]

Skolimowski's work offers a ripe template for understanding the way nature serves as the backdrop to community. Similar to Bellah's appeal for a moral ecology, Skolimowski advocates for healing our minds and souls by recognizing our responsibility to others and to the earth as a condition of the human experience. Recognizing this truth encourages the personal development of ecological values: the earth is home to our homes. Caring for the planet should be akin to maintaining your lawn when viewed through this lens. Eco-philosophy tenets ask us to consider our relationship with the earth and the ways place informs our sense of self, our connection to others, and our responsibility to the environment at large.

People love to refer to particular places as spiritual in nature. Personally, I love the beach. Tapping into feelings of well-being and connection is easier for me when I am watching the waves break along the sandy shore. Some people love to hike. The silence of the forest gives rise to an internal sense of peacefulness. And, of course, there is no shortage of special, man-made places that resonate with awe-inducing feelings. Think of Roman ruins, Egyptian pyramids, Stonehenge, or the Golden Gate Bridge, just to name a few. But I sometimes wonder what the world might look like if we all worked a bit harder to see the beauty in every place, to take responsibility not just for our trash but for the *resonant feelings* we leave behind in spaces.

As John Mayer famously sang in his iconic ode to millennials everywhere: "It's hard to be persistent / When we're standing at a distance / So, we keep waiting (waiting) / Waiting on the world to change."[6] His song reminds me of a funny purchase I once made at a quirky little shop in Fairfield, Iowa: a jar of honey that came in a "singing" box. When you opened the packaging, the box "sang" a little ditty about "heaven descending." While it made me smile, it also made me question how we will ever transform the world if we remain fixated on heaven coming to us. Don't we need to see and imagine a little heaven right here, right now, every day, in order to slowly grow its existence?

---

5. Skolimowski, *A Sacred Place to Dwell*, 4.

6. John Mayer, "Waiting on the World to Change," *Continuum* (Aware/Columbia Records, 2006).

Revitalizing Detroit

There is a clear relationship between our perception of different spaces and the activities we expect to see there, just as we have preconceived ideas about the interactions we can expect to have with people in various different settings. For example, if you go to a water park, an oversized inflatable swan tube may not be an unexpected sight. However, if said swan ended up being offered as a mode of transportation to ferry you across a lake, you might feel a bit surprised! I knew a young man who got into a punch-throwing conflict one time. Despite his insistence of innocence, it was eventually revealed that the fight had happened in the parking lot of a 7-11, at two in the morning, shortly after he had taken a baseball bat out of the trunk of his car. While an inflatable swan tube plus a waterslide likely equals fun, combining a late night with a baseball bat and a 7-11 parking lot might not be the best idea.

Reframing the expected activities taking place in communities takes some creative thought. Detroit serves as an ideal locale to play around with concepts of space and place. In his award-winning 2010 book, *Reimagining Detroit: Opportunities for Redefining an American City*, John Gallagher, journalist for the *Detroit Free Press*, wrote about the unique opportunities presented by a city with approximately forty vacant square miles.[7] Detroit, the former "Paris of the New World," suffered significant urban decay during the second half of the twentieth century as a result of numerous factors, including economic decline, the 1968 race riots, and a mass exodus to the suburbs. Rather than documenting the problems present in modern-day Detroit, Gallagher writes about the innovative community-building work happening in the city and offers a blueprint for "what can be" with a reconceived concept of city living. And, indeed, for those of us who live in Detroit, examples of the vibrant work Gallagher describes abound.

Years ago, I had a group of CCS students who took it upon themselves to plant pansies in a vacant lot close to school. This was before the advent of community gardens becoming "a thing" in Detroit. I can't help but wonder what role those fierce little pansies played in the process. I also had a group of students leave "signs of love" on abandoned buildings

---

7. John Gallagher, *Reimagining Detroit: Opportunities for Redefining an American City* (Detroit: Wayne State University Press, 2010).

across the city. Frankly, as much as I got a kick out of their enthusiasm, I had my doubts about the impact of that project. Yet, now—some years later—I can't help but scratch my head in happy confusion when I see images of Detroit's famous vacant train station celebrated in glossy photography magazines.

One of my favorite Detroit-based projects, the "Mobile Anagama," happens to be spearheaded by a former student. Henry Crissman, a ceramicist, fervently believes in a relationship between personal creativity, social responsibility, and connectivity. During graduate school at Alfred University, Henry's thesis project was to develop a moveable kiln with the intent to use it as a "sort of public art space where people come together to celebrate the process of making something beautiful."[8]

Making pottery in unexpected places is a good example of positive repatterning of activity expectations. Henry's art lives within a socially interactive framework. Firing up the kiln becomes a neighborhood celebration and a living example of some combination of Skolimowski's philosophy, Lippard's thesis, and Gallagher's practical advice. "Listen, this isn't just about me and my work," Henry said. "This is really about reimagining space. I mean, how many people get to fire up a community kiln in their driveway?" Art is a verb in Henry's mind—it signifies action, process, connectivity, and joy. Henry believes there needs to be a shift in our collective understanding of the power of art and its connection to community bonds, celebration, and interaction.

Henry's passion for ceramics is infectious. You can't help but have a good time in his presence. There is a certain ceremonial aspect to working with clay. As Henry says, "It is impossible to explain because I only confuse myself and my audience but there is something about the invisible cord that ties every moment seamlessly together. All I know is that it is bigger than me. It just pulls me along creating this thing that in the end looks like a cup but is really the outgrowth of a million tiny moments of interaction with the clay." That invisible force that moves Henry somehow moves his audience too—community members playing with clay invariably "catch" the feelings of good, clean fun. Makes you wonder how the echo of all that activity reverberates out into the community, transforming spaces into places of meaning.

---

8. Henry Crissman, accessed October 18, 2018, https://www.henrycrissman.com/#/the-mobile-anagama/.

Student Paper:
Alexis—Home Is a Place of Limitless Potential

My personal identity has been influenced by the place I call home. From a very young age, I found that my parents were the happiest when I entertained myself close to home. While much of their motivation may have been overly protective, I have found that it has served me well. Home, for me, is a place of limitless potential.

Our neighborhood consists of a small group of homes built around a small lake. In a way, the lake is a part of me. I have raised a family of ducks on the lake. In the winter, when the lake freezes over, I feed them daily. Many nights, I go to bed hearing the geese squawking away. In the morning, I wake to the sound of the birds and various other critters who call the lake home.

Once when I was about twelve years old, I witnessed an event so magical that it will forever be engraved on my soul. The happening was so unreal, so shocking and slightly terrifying, that I have wondered over the years if I have exaggerated the memory of it—but, honestly, I don't think so.

The event took place on a beautiful, clear summer day. My friend Claire and I had been playing outside all afternoon. We were sharing a great adventure due to the fact that a tiny island had spontaneously popped up not far from the shore. Exposed by a dryer than usual summer, the island became a private oasis for Claire and me. A favorite activity of ours was to float on a raft to the island. While there, we would feed the baby fish, poke sticks in the mud, and pretend to build a camp.

We traveled back and forth between the shore of the lake and the island dozens of times on that fateful day. Shortly after returning from the island at dusk, we felt the wind begin to pick up. Out of nowhere, the sky just shifted, the wind howled, and a wave of water ran up the beach. Paper and other light objects blew toward the water. Then, the most incredible thing happened. The water on the right side of the lake began to swirl. It quickly grew into a larger swirl that almost appeared as a drain in the center of the lake. It happened so quickly. It felt like watching a tornado from above—absolutely mesmerizing! My friend and I stood at the edge of the water, frozen in dumbfounded awe with our hair blowing like crazy. It only took a minute. The second we caught our breaths we started screaming and ran straight to the garage, where my dad was working, completely unaware of the magic that had just transpired in our backyard.

Dear Alexis—

Ohhhh, I love this story!

As a child you lived a life at the intuitive edge, seeking grace in your play and magic in your interactions. It seems that you recognize the beauty in the world around you in sincere ways— and you are not afraid to share your enthusiasm for the richness of life. The fact that you have managed to maintain that sense of wonder in your everyday life is inspiring.

Love the magic of the story at the lake. I have a similar tale that makes no objective sense but provides me with a sense of peace that I find comfort in. A few years ago, I was taking a walk around a small pond in Glen Arbor, Michigan. It was a beautiful day. Lost in my own thoughts, I noticed that a swan was following me around the pond while I walked. In a very literal way, I tested him. If I stopped, he stopped. If I walked forward, he glided forward. If I stepped back, he swam back. At the very instant that I became utterly mesmerized by the phenomenon, I recognized that there was a beaver slapping his tail while floating on his back next to the swan. And, as I looked up, I saw two deer run by, a rabbit hop past my feet, and a swarm of beautiful birds pass overhead. It was utterly, totally, spellbindingly magical. Took my breath away—I mean, you can't make this stuff up, right? It was like being inside a living painting!

In class, we've spent quite a bit of time discussing the way art-making and design is connected to our personal identity. In your next draft, I think you can delve more deeply into how the incident at the lake affected your identity. I specifically remember your comment about using tiny feathers as an application to shoes being related to your affection for whimsy, magic, and fantasy. Reading your paper, I cannot help but wonder if that inclination may be rooted in your experiences as a child at the lake. I have a creative writing assignment for you to undertake as you finish up this paper. I want you to imagine yourself as an aspect of the natural landscape watching your little-girl self. In other words, pick a tree, or a cloud, or a sturdy flower standing tall on the shore on the day of your great adventure. Retell the story of Alexis growing into herself through the voice of that long-ago, silent witness. My hunch is that this writing exercise will reveal new truths about yourself and why you like what you like, believe what you believe, and, maybe, why you are so enchanted by the idea of tiny, hot-pink feathers adorning high-heeled pumps!

Recognizing the magic in the world will ensure that you grow the experience. Everything in our universe aches to be seen as beautiful. This is why you are so capable of creating beautiful objects—because you yourself see the beauty and tease it out of the materials you work with. Your presence literally enlivens the physicality of the material you work with. What a gift!

Love,

Molly

Twelfth Week

What Does It Mean to Be a Consumer?

Television commercials are a form of religious literature . . . Like all religious parables they put forward a concept of sin, intimations of the way to redemption, and a vision of Heaven. They also suggest what are the roots of evil and what are the obligations of the holy.

—Neil Postman

Clearly, You Need Eyedrops

Imagine you frequently wake up with itchy, burning, red eyes. A trip to the doctor reveals that you don't have an infection. It is not allergy season. And so, despite your discomfort, you "get the red out" via drugstore eyedrops. One day it occurs to you that your eyes seem to be reddest on Tuesday, with decreasing itchiness as the week progresses. You ask your wife, "Hey, honey, do you ever notice that your eyes bother you on Tuesdays?"

She smiles and says "No," handing you the Visine as she ventures off to work.

The following week, on a Tuesday, you happen to be chatting with your neighbor when he suddenly starts rubbing his eyes like a madman. Surprised, you ask, "Ted, do you happen to notice your eyes bother you on Tuesdays more than any other day?"

He pauses—looks at you like you are crazy—and then shakes his head and says, "Now that you mention it, yes. And, would you believe we had to keep little Teddy home from school last Tuesday and Wednesday due to itchy, red eyes and a raw, angry throat?"

Together, you and Ted begin to question your neighbors. In house after house, you find individuals suffering from similar symptoms. Eventually, you knock on the door of a lawyer neither of you have ever met. She immediately welcomes you into her home, exclaiming, "I have been waiting for you! Did you know that the tire company located just one mile away burns discarded rubber every Tuesday? There is a group of environmentalists concerned about the impact on air quality. We want to file a class action suit to stop this harmful practice. We need community support to make our case."

Solving individual problems by "shopping" for solutions—Visine to the rescue!—is an American habit related to an outsized emphasis on our role as consumers. While I intend no disrespect to the makers of Visine, sometimes we need to look beyond our individually driven solutions to the broader societal issues that may be causing the problems in the first place.

Dare to Be Different

In America, the quintessential consumer culture, purchasing power is linked to identity in a meaningful way. Last fall, I visited High Point, North Carolina. Home to a multitude of furniture makers, High Point hosts a twice-yearly "market" that caters to shop owners, interior designers, and others that work in the design industry. If you're lucky, like me, you can go to the show as the guest of one of these industry insiders. My own trip coincided with a home renovation project. On the day of the trip, I carefully chose my "outfit"—casual and comfortable but befitting of my social status: a cashmere sweater, Citizen straight-leg jeans, and leather Prada loafers. Arriving at the merchandise market for sale day, I felt as if I was wandering in a carnival fun house. Everywhere I looked, there I was! I looked exactly like everyone else in my surprisingly (at least to me!) unoriginal, affluent, middle-aged, white-woman-gone-shopping "costume."

The reading that most unnerves my students is likely Raymond Williams's "Advertising: The Magic System."[1] Sitting in class decked out in whatever "hot" fashion item is the current trend, my students routinely

---

1. Raymond Williams, "Advertising: The Magic System," in *Media Studies: A Reader*, ed. Paul Marris and Sue Thornham (Edinburgh: Edinburgh University Press, 1999).

deny that advertising plays any role in their fashion choices. While it is not typically part of my repertoire to laugh "at" young people, sometimes I find I must bite my lip as I gaze out at my Mac-tapping, ripped-de-signer-jean-wearing, Starbucks-drinking audience. Like it or not, I gently admonish them, we are all influenced by advertising.

Williams begins his essay by asserting the irony that individuals are not generally all that materialist. If they were, there would be no need to attach false meanings to products—Coke and love, Coors and fun times, or Apple and cool. Having our needs met through false association is a primary requirement of a consumer culture. Whereas religion once provided a framework of meaning, the turn of the twentieth century brought with it a new emphasis on consumption. Modern advertisers learned to tap into the increasing anxiety about the fast-changing culture by linking human emotional needs with purchasing prowess. Today, it is an accepted belief that we fulfill our emotional needs via buying and consuming. Historian Jackson Lears refers to this phenomenon as the "therapeutic ethos."

The key point of Williams's article is to illuminate this "cultural pattern in which objects in of themselves are not enough but must be validated—even if only in fantasy—by association and personal meanings which in *a different culture pattern* might be more directly available" (italics mine).[2] Williams refers to this as "magic" and compares it to the magical systems that exist in "simpler societies," finding it a rather strange occurrence in our highly developed, scientifically and technologically advanced society. Advertising—consumerism's partner in crime and very best friend—operates to preserve the ideal of having one's needs met by buying goods and services. We do not so much buy a chair as much as we buy the confirmation of our minimalist sensibilities (think sleek, steel design). We do not buy a car—we buy status and empowerment. And so it goes.

Williams argues that our identity as consumers creates a marketplace society where individuals are essentially the "channels through which products flow and disappear."[3] In all our modes of communication—think of my red-eyed friend treating his burning eyes with Visine—we confirm and confirm again our dependency on the marketplace and our role as

2. Williams, "Advertising: the Magic System," 462.

3. Williams, "Advertising: The Magic System," 463.

a consumer. It's as if the undercurrent of all our choice-making is the following: "I have a problem. This problem can be solved via my personal purchasing power."

Additionally, our identification as consumers shapes our social relationships. In his book *A Theater of Envy: William Shakespeare*, French literary theorist René Girard argues that individuals desire what others desire. This "mimetic desire" means we imitate others' desires in a way that simultaneously both draws us together and pulls us apart. As Girard writes, "Individuals who desire the same thing are united by something so powerful that, as long as they can share whatever they desire, they remain the best of friends; as soon as they cannot, they become the worst of enemies."[4] In a consumer society that constantly stokes our desire for innumerable different objects in order to keep profits flowing, our relationships may be disproportionately influenced by mimetic desire, which both bonds us and increases the potential for strife and dissatisfaction.

This reality leads to a multitude of questions, the first and most important of which is to consider the purpose of society. Williams, a Marxist theorist and advocate for socialism, does not believe that the private sector can fulfill the needs of society as a whole. In fact, he proposes that if we identified more as "users" than "consumers," our collective effort would be more inclined toward the building of community parks and hospitals, the protection of natural resources, and the maintenance of our schools. As consumers, however, we are mesmerized by the glory of shining, new objects popping up all over the place.

As a lover of beautiful things, an admitted shoe hoarder, and the daughter of an advertising executive, I find myself stumped by this conundrum. Where do we go from here? Are we even aware of the ways that we curate our identities via our purchasing choices? How do we disentangle appropriate consumption from gluttony? I mean, if all this consuming was leaving us fat and happy, I'd say, let's run with it! But, evidence-based statistics seem to confirm that we are mostly just fat and unhappy. Our collective commitment to maintaining the status quo is embedded in our habits, routines, and ignorance of advertising's ability to manufacture desire and make us think it is our own. As Don Juan tells Carlos Castaneda in *Tales of Power*, "So, in essence, the world that your reason wants to sus-

---

4. René Girard, *A Theater of Envy: William Shakespeare* (South Bend, IN: St. Augustine's Press, 1991), 3.

tain is the world created by a description and its dogmatic and inviolable rules, which the reason learns to accept and defend."[5]

I've struggled more with this chapter than any other. Like my fellow Americans, I am so embedded in the web of consumerism it is difficult to imagine an alternative pattern of living. And, frankly, I'm not so sure the answer lies in a complete rejection of capitalism. Irony of ironies, I might argue that we need a rebranding of American culture. Perhaps we ought to employ the old "stop, look, and listen" rule that is offered to toddlers looking to cross the street. A momentary pause before we swipe our cards, and some consideration of the way we erroneously attempt to fill our infinite emptiness with finite pieces of stuff. And, last but not least, listening to our internal voices rather than outer expectations.

One last anecdote: As a child, I had a recurring dream that "I" was one piece of an assembly line (swear to God!). Trust me, it's an odd sensation to feel yourself hanging as a component piece of a production line. Given that I grew up in Detroit and visited the Ford assembly plant every couple of years on field trips, I wrote the dream off as a strange trick of the mind. In his book *A Sacred Place to Dwell*, Henryk Skolimowski poses the question of what the world looks like if it is conceived of as a mere machine. Now, I wonder if my childhood dream was my own answer to that question, representing my own interpretation of how it felt to grow up in a consumer culture.

I found some validation in sociologist George Ritzer's book *The McDonaldization of Society*.[6] Using principles such as efficiency, calculability, uniformity, and control, Ritzer outlines the ways "McDonaldization" impacts social relations, interactional dynamics, and the "feel" of our culture. In other words, the way American society has adopted the values of fast-food culture: quick service, limited choices, and, as some of my students have been quick to quip during this lesson, a red-headed "Donald" as our chief executive!

Ritzer's comments regarding higher education strike a personal chord: "Students may feel like little more than objects into which knowledge is poured as they move along an information-providing and degree-granting educational assembly line."[7] The "vocational" or outcome-oriented bent

---

5. Carlos Castaneda, *Tales of Power* (New York: Washington Square Press, 1991), 98.

6. George Ritzer, *The McDonaldization of Society* (Thousand Oaks, CA: Sage, 1993).

7. Ritzer, *The McDonaldization of Society*, 158.

of our education system comes directly from our capitalist social system. Education is a reflection of the system as a whole, and in turn it feeds the system. If you're taught that what is valued are skills that result directly in profits or a product being created, that's what you will believe to be valuable. What if our education system emphasized different values—like seeking meaning in what we learn, finding connections between different disciplines, and understanding learning as a lifelong process? Students might grow up to want to change the system to reflect those values.

My long-ago dream was a child's confirmation of the impact of our current, consumer reality on our collective emotional state. The numbing reality of recognizing yourself as a cog in the assembly line of life is depressing. Like the air rushing out of a popped balloon, it immediately forces you to reconsider how you have constructed your identity. This week's lesson leaves my students feeling quiet. They typically shuffle out of the room in thoughtful ambiguity.

To Be Seen

Several years ago, a photography student asked me if I would participate in her photo series for senior studio. Flattered to be asked, I immediately agreed. For years, I have worn bright red lipstick in the hopes of being discovered like Lana Turner at the corner drugstore. On the appointed day of the shoot, I packed a bag of potential outfits, blew out my hair, and painted on my lips.

As soon as I arrived, Jen invited me to look at some of the images she had already completed for her thesis project. The first image was of her father. He was seated on an unmade bed with his colostomy bag exposed. The second was of a young man collapsed in an overstuffed chair—his tie loosened, his face grim, Las Vegas glittering through the glass window behind him. And, so it went: an overweight woman with candy circling her head, a video gamer hidden in a basement. You get the gist.

Looking at the series of pictures, panic slowly set in. I suddenly felt confused as to how or why Jen thought I belonged with this rag-tag group of individuals sharing their raw vulnerability. Not wanting to offend her, I figured I'd put on my most slimming black dress and let her take a few pictures just to humor her. Prior to taking the picture, she asked me to jot down a thought on my greatest fear. I spontaneously wrote: "Sometimes,

I wonder if there is anything left that is worth saying; while words may echo, it is feeling that resonates."

Jen ended up winning "student select" for her project. Her blown-up photos graced the entryway to the senior show. Despite their prominent position at the show and my attendance, not one single person recognized my portrait. The image, taken through a long lens, showed me holding my notes and speaking into the loneliness of an empty auditorium. Even my husband looked away dismissively at first glance. Jen had captured a moment of deep feeling. Even my carefully applied makeup, slimming dress, and good cover story could not hide my true vulnerability. In asking me to reveal my fear, Jen had set an intention. Her talent and patient eye unearthed the truth of my being.

Reflecting on my participation in Jen's project, I blush just a bit at initially desiring a "glamor shot." That desire, I now recognize, comes from living in a culture in which much of our daily appearance is an advertisement for who we think the world wants to see. In the end, I feel a certain pride at being a member of this brave group of individuals willing to share and embrace their true vulnerability. It has taken me several years to look honestly at that photo—to see my truth exposed.

Student Paper:
Madison—Caught without a Sequential Occupation Strategy

Success is relative. My artistic interests and concerns have been in a state of flux from the time I started my education, but have become more concentrated since I began to meditate. Increasingly, I am feeling a strong desire to live my life the way I choose to live it, not in strict accordance with outside perspectives.

In my fifth year at the College for Creative Studies, I am becoming acquainted with parts of myself that I haven't much thought about before, and that I surely wouldn't have come to know had it not been for some of the courses I've taken here. This introspective awakening is where my attention has been directed, and it has allowed me to tap into things creatively that I was not prepared to access. This has dramatically affected my creative work. As I approach the end of my schooling experience, I am better able to recognize and acknowledge where my propensities—and my values as an artist rather than a capitalist—lie. Nevertheless, at what is apparently the moment of truth, I have been caught without a sequential occupation strategy. All my dreamy, abstract notions of success seem to be fighting with the expectations of my friends, family, and landlord.

At twenty-four, the only thing I have totally figured out is that it's actually pretty normal for me to have . . . nothing figured out. It's something most of the people in my life generally agree with, but demonstrating it to them seems to elicit a kind of awkwardly insinuated disappointment in me. "Follow your heart" and "who cares what everyone else thinks" are lovely sentiments, but they always seem to be spoken passively, or in an indistinct way. I am worried by the idea that I am not able to identify my own definition of success. This boundless feeling of insecurity leaves me paralyzed in the face of contemplating next steps.

My boyfriend is one person who supports me unconditionally and understands my conflict, and I believe this is because he is an artist himself. He reassures me regularly, explaining that not only is the experience of having gone through four years of college valuable in itself, but that preoccupation with "making it big" will probably only establish limits to which I just might not be ready to adapt at this time in my life.

I feel that there is an element of humility missing from the contemporary art world. I think this stems from a misplaced enthusiasm to get ahead in it. It is the expectation in our society that every talent or category of intelligence be made profitable by way of obtrusiveness and self-absorption presented as intense passion.

In a society in which a person's value is generally measured by accumulations of wealth, I am finding it increasingly difficult to share this cultural perception of success. I suppose this is an ironic attitude considering that I'm paying tens of thousands of dollars to attend a college whose main responsibility is to provide me with a promising future in a field I chose for myself as an idealistic nineteen year old.

I am sometimes overcome with fear that failure truly does lie in veering off on the path I've already set—that not having internships, awards, profitable social connections, and solo exhibitions under my belt before the end of my academic career is indicative of my own lack of drive, and foreshadows a bleak future toiling away in a factory or something. I am frustrated with my own anxiety because I know that the idea of success is a social construct and that no outcome in life is certain. I know that I shouldn't feel condemned to underachievement. In truth, I don't even really know what I'd like to achieve. I only know that I want to create and grow in my own way and somehow manage to keep *my inner world* awake.

Dear Madison—

First off, it is okay not to know what you want to do. In fact, it may even be an advantageous way to feel, as it ensures your openness to possibility. At the very end of *The Book of Secrets* by Deepak Chopra, he offers the following three question/answer sets:

> *Who am I?* You are the totality of the universe acting through a human nervous system.
> *Where did I come from?* You came from a source that was never born and will never die.
> *Why am I here?* To create the world in every moment.[8]

He says these questions are the most important questions any teacher can offer a student. These are the questions that open all the doors. I think I agree.

Your comments regarding the challenges of finding success outside the "predisposed perception of success" echo the fact that your work challenges the systems that exist in the world today. I happen to think this is exciting. However, I recognize that it can be a lonely road to travel. I recently stumbled upon a lovely idea put forth by psychologist James Hillman: Art as a visible manifestation of the "soul's desperate concerns."[9] Perhaps, following this logic, the new aesthetics will not be found in museums or objects but in connective interactional processes. In other words, perhaps (as you allude to in your paper) the only thing left to design is the designer himself. Of course, we can see the enormity of the misuse of this concept in the incredible emphasis on branding the individual. Branding does not heal the soul. Our entire mode of thinking must change— and this is where the power of transcendence enters. Expanding our consciousness literally enlivens our imagination, grows our compassion, and enhances our morality. It seems to me this is the new aesthetics that the world needs now.

---

8. Deepak Chopra, *The Book of Secrets* (London: Ebury Publishing, 2009), 262.
9. Suzi Gablik, *The Reenchantment of Art* (New York: Thames and Hudson, 1992), 114.

Have you ever heard of the novel *Dhalgren*?[10] A former student shared it with me a few years ago. The book takes place in a surreal, postapocalyptic city called Bellona—supposedly the author, Samuel R. Delany, took inspiration from Detroit. Anyhoo—at one point in the book, a wannabe writer is offered a magic shield to aid in his quest. On one side of the shield is written: "Be true to yourself that you may be true to your work." On the other is written: "Be true to your work that you may be true to yourself." While I seem to be out of magic shields this week, I thought the advice might help. These two goals may be more connected than you realize.

As you mention in your paper, "figuring it all out" is a rather lofty goal. Of the billions of people who have come before, we have no evidence that anyone has managed to crawl out of that rabbit hole with a definitive answer yet. The true secret of the "grown-up world" is that we are all just faking it. Some of us just happen to be better at it than others. Every day when I pull into my driveway, I think, "How can it be that I am the 'lady' of this manor?!" Aging is such a funny phenomenon—most days it seems utterly impossible that I've lived on this earth for fifty years! And, yet, there is great evidence that I have actually grown up. That evidence is my almost-grown-up children, the parade of students who have walked through my life, and memories of trips, parties, and accomplishments. That said, internally I feel the same—aging has not diminished my curiosity, my enthusiasm, or my sense of innocence.

There are great joys related to aging. Without sounding too cliché, wisdom goes hand in hand with maturity. The practical experiences life tosses your way—paying bills, raising kids, organizing events, caring for parents, even yard work, etc.— tend to school you on the importance of staying organized, maintaining relationships, and being honest. This may sound "boring," but in truth, figuring out how to live an ethically driven life lends itself to really limiting the stress you feel on a day-to-day basis. And stress reduction leads to happiness. And, happiness . . . well, that's what it's all about, right?

---

10. Samuel R. Delany, *Dhalgren* (New York: Bantam Books, 1975).

My hunch is that life will continue to tug you along. In embracing a creative way of living, you will find new opportunities. The elusive "career" you dream of will happen whether you will it to or not—you will meet people, take jobs, and keep on keepin' on. Cultivating a spirit of creative effort will foster the development of a rich and meaningful life. Trust in the flow of life, Madison.

Much love,

Molly

Thirteenth Week

What Does It Mean to Be an Artist?

There is a solitude of space
A solitude of sea
A solitude of death, but these
Society shall be
Compared with that profounder site
That polar privacy
A soul admitted to itself—
Finite infinity.

—Emily Dickinson

A Pie-in-the-Sky Health Clinic

Several years ago, I was invited to attend a critique in the interior design department at CCS. We met at a large conference table on a sunny day in the spring. Each student spoke for approximately ten minutes, sharing a vision board and the various materials they had picked for a proposed health center. All the students possessed the social acumen to give a strong presentation. They offered justifications for material, color, and other design choices. But, at the end of the presentation, when asked questions about the types of services offered at the clinic or the type of patient they envisioned visiting the clinic, they were stumped. Each of them had designed a pie-in-the-sky clinic—an imaginary building that existed outside the constraints of community expectation, need, or limitation. This anecdote speaks to the limits of education in a vacuum. How do we teach students to change the world if we don't also teach them the value of reading the world?

I offer this story as an example of the importance of examining our cultural model in order to understand how it affects the way we think and determines the way we work. While this group of young designers had spent months making sure they understood the physical dimensions of the project, not one of them had considered the mission of the clinic itself. Additionally, the competition between individual students created an atmosphere of one-upsmanship that, frankly, led to certain indulgent choices that likely would not be appropriate for a standard health clinic. When asked about this, one student timidly suggested she be "graded on the idea that her clinic be recognized as part of a concierge health care model." In truth, this was a fair suggestion. One, I had to agree, that worked. That said, the afternoon provided me with this gnawing sense at the edge of my awareness that something about these presentations was ever so slightly "off."

Creativity Is Intimacy

As a child, I lived in fear of the shoe-box diorama assignment. In short, I stink at art. Ironic, when you consider that I've spent my teaching career working with art and design students. But, here's the thing: I love beauty. And I especially love people who can create beautiful objects. I stand in awe of creative talent. The joy it brings me to think I might positively influence my students' artistic endeavors is immense. That said, over the years, I've thought a lot about what it means to be an artist. I mean, just because I can't sew, or paint or bead or draw, does that mean I am not an artist at heart?

As a sociologist, I have always been interested in the intersection between art and culture. In graduate school, I wrote a lengthy research paper on what factors determine the value of an artist's work. In fact, there is a whole body of research devoted to understanding how art is valued. Value, it turns out, is more frequently related to relationships sur-rounding an object than the object itself. Whole networks of relationships sustain the art world; gallerists, collectors, and critics can make or break an individual artist. It's as if certain members of society carry fairy wands capable of conferring status to "real" artists and the art pieces themselves.

My first "teaching" gig was leading gallery tours. The mission of my tours was to offer everyday folk the confidence to look at/enjoy/interact with art from a place of true connection. To this end, I employed the "Black Turtleneck Rule." The "rule"—which wasn't actually a rule, but it sounded cool—was established as a disarming technique, and I would share it at the beginning of all my walking tours. "The Black Turtleneck rule," I would tell my audiences, "refers to the feeling of intimidation one feels in the presence of the black-turtleneck-wearing, cooler-than-cool gallery worker. You know the feeling," I would joke with them, "You are standing out on the street facing a larger-than-life glass door rimmed in shiny steel. You gaze longingly at the images lit from behind inside that sleek space, desperate to enter but terrified of being questioned about your taste, knowledge, or opinions. For crying out loud, you just want something to match your sofa!" Everyone would laugh and laugh, saying, "Oh, yes, yes, yes—that IS how it feels! Looking at art is a terribly intimating experience." The whole point was to get these people to think about how they had been conditioned to think they were not capable of recognizing, evaluating, or appreciating art—and to start questioning that conditioning.

While this is not an art history book—and I am certainly not an art historian—indulge me for just a moment or two: History is littered with a plethora of definitions of art, paradigm-shifting ideas about the nature of creativity, and the rapidly changing attitudes of artists themselves. Art has always served as a mirror reflecting the times. We know that in ancient cultures, art was anonymous, as the concept of individuality did not yet exist. But unsurprisingly, individualism has been at the heart of our modern understanding of art for centuries.

The philosopher Immanuel Kant laid the foundation for how art and art making have been understood in the Western world for the past 250 years. The openness to experience art, according to Kant, must be devoid of any concept, emotion, or even interest in the object. For Kant, standards of beauty were, at the deepest level, absolute and universal. Beauty was something one felt and recognized with some immediacy due to the purity of form, because beauty and truth existed in the same "beyond." The relationship between art and moral goodness defined beauty. In other words, when you look at truly beautiful object, you can tell it is truly beautiful because you realize that it is good. Kant's definition offered humanity a sense of harmony in the commonality of experience when interacting with art. It also drove a wedge between art and observer (that same wedge the

Enlightenment drove between the knower and the known, which we so often see getting in the way of meaningful understanding in education) and kept artists elevated to a special status. As you can imagine, the ability to pull from an absolute source of moral goodness rendered artists divinely inspired individuals. In fact, Kant referred to them as "geniuses," a word we still use today to describe creators of moving, magnificent works.

Kant's absolutes regarding beauty have offered art critics, historians, collectors, and makers fertile ground for debate for the past 250 years. Up until the pop art phenomenon, art generally developed in a linear fashion. From impressionism to fauvism, from surrealism to abstract expressionism, art followed a developmental path that echoed the progression of society. Over the last several hundred years, artists have moved from imitating nature and life with more and more accuracy to exploring the potential of materials and the limits of surface. After the development of the camera, artists were freed to express new forms of feeling, ideas, and, importantly, themselves.

This steady development of expression and further abstraction culminated with Andy Warhol's celebrated Brillo box as sculpture (1964), which effectively posed the question: "What is art?" The point being, of course, that if we cannot distinguish between the Brillo box under the kitchen sink and the one on a pedestal in the Stable Gallery, how are we to recognize art in any distinguishable pattern? And so, in the 1960s, art, like culture, exploded. The boundaries between art and everyday life diminished. As the French philosopher Jean Baudrillard wrote, contemporary culture in its obsessive visual context produced "the end of interiority and intimacy, the overexposure and transparence of the world."[1] In our modern culture of commodified artistic production, visual representations began to propagate at an accelerating rate in recursive, self-referential cycles that ultimately reduced them to meaninglessness. Piecing things back together requires a reframing of the definition of "art" and "artist."

Kant's ideal of absolute beauty holds limited power in the modern art world. But the sliver of relevance Kant's philosophy maintains is the celebration of individually based creative talent. In other words, some people are born to make art, and others are born to recognize art. Hmm . . . that leaves an awful lot of us out of the art equation.

---

1. Jean Baudrillard, "The Ecstasy of Communication," in *The Anti-Aesthetic: Essays on Postmodern Culture*, ed. Hal Foster (New York: New Press, 1998), 153.

And, so, back to my lovely interior design students. Creating meaningful work requires that we move beyond merely expressing ourselves and toward offering a vision that connects with others. As Suzi Gablik writes in her book *The Reenchantment of Art*, "In modern society, artists see themselves as quintessential free agents, pursuing their own ends. Our cultural myths support economic advancement and the hard-edged individualist writ large, rather than service, caring attitudes and participation. Though certain individuals are exploring and implementing more communal values, others have not shifted their understanding in this way and may not wish to. For them, art remains a question of radical autonomy."[2] This individualistic, "look-at-me" feeling was exactly what I sensed during that health clinic design critique.

"Look at me" and "look at this" insist that art makers and art viewers remain separate from the object of their design or admiration. The art object validates the creative individual, or the creative individual validates the art. Meaning lies in the observed or the observer rather than in the integration of the two. Seeing beyond the individual perspective requires expansive consciousness. This is one more reason meditation in the classroom is so valuable. It helps the artist engage in creative work from a space of integration.

In the early 1960s, Marghanita Laski set out to discover if the arts simply made people better or if they actually provided individuals with a distinctive experience. In her landmark study, *Ecstasy*, Laski theorized that the ecstatic feeling that accompanies viewing or making art is associated with the spontaneous organizing power of the mind.[3] Laski's work supports the notion that there exists a connection between the feelings of unity and meaningful creative work. In other words, creativity at its finest level is celebrated in intimacy. It is the merging of the poet with the poem, the potter with the clay, the painter with the canvas, or the designer with the space that allows one to experience an expanded sense of creative ecstasy. This is the mesmerizing moment of beauty that exists in the space of forgetting oneself only to connect with the infinite beyond.

Several years ago, I had a student obsessed with floral photography. In his artist statement, he wrote about his desire to become "closer and

---

2. Suzi Gablik, *The Reenchantment of Art* (New York: Thames and Hudson, 1992), 116.

3. Marghanita Laski, *Ecstasy: A Study of Some Secular and Religious Experiences* (London: Cresset, 1965).

closer to nature and understand the visual, emotional, and scientific details of the flower." In order to bring the finest level of attention to the flower, my advice to him was to be devoted to his meditation practice.

In my letter to him at the end of the semester, I wrote, "True understanding of the flower will come when you find you have established true unity with your subject. Complete detachment from results will help this to naturally occur. In that moment, you will see/feel/hear the very flow of life moving through the flower—you will begin to literally 'live' the flower. Reflections of beauty that come from that space will not be clouded by ambition, expectation, or ego, they will simply manifest as they ARE. Capturing that level of truth and beauty will be the great gift you can offer the universe—and the light that beams out from those images will gracefully fall back upon you with gratitude. Immersing oneself in expanded experiences of reflection furthers creativity from a space of awareness."

There is a famous geneticist by the name of Barbara McClintock. She won a Nobel Prize for her research. I read an interesting critique of her work recently that I thought was relevant to this conversation. McClintock "gained valuable knowledge by empathizing with her corn plants. By submersing herself in their world, she was able to dissolve boundaries between the observer and the observed."[4] This dissolution of boundaries is the art of great science and the goal of meditation. Reading about McClintock's work and thinking about my flower-obsessed student validated my efforts to bring meditation to my art and design students.

What does it mean to be an artist? To me, being an artist or living a creative life is defined by the ability to see the unity in the diversity all around us. True creatives operate by seeing themselves in others and growing the goodness that runs between them. This connection encourages a "participating consciousness" rather than an observing one. It is less about "look at me" or "look at that" and more about "look at us." A participating consciousness celebrates otherness, strives toward compassion, and relinquishes competition. This is a kind of visionary or artistic way of seeing the world that creates true grace.

Engagement with the world around us and true connection to other people is what will help us evolve our art-making capability. This type

---

4. Daniel P. Barbezat and Mirabai Bush, *Contemplative Practices in Higher Education: Powerful Methods to Transform Teaching and Learning* (San Francisco: Jossey-Bass, 2014), ix.

of engagement kicks tired definitions of "what is art" to the curb. The black-turtleneck-wearing expert no longer intimidates lovers of art. The power of the "gaze" equalizes by resting in the space between the viewer and the object of desire. Most importantly, we recognize art making as intangible sport. It can be interactional in nature and no longer limited to the creation of practical handicraft, performance, or design. Art making can happen at the grocery store when you see, complement, and rejoice in the presence of a new baby. Artful interaction infuses the world with the healing power of love. No longer are our failed shoe-box dioramas indicative of our art-making capacity!

Onto the Silver Screen

Over the years, I have developed close relationships with a few of my students. Our time together occasionally extends beyond the classroom to include a cup of coffee or a series of emails after graduation. There is one student, however, who won my heart forever. Writing about her now, I find tears streaming unbidden down my face. My own children occasionally accuse me of loving Chelsea more than I love them. I readily admit that it's easier to love the child you did not have the burden of seeing through the teenage years. And, believe me, Chelsea likely would have done me in with her rebellious spirit, simmering anger, and outrageous courage to test boundaries. As mother and daughter, we would have been a toxic mix. As teacher and student, we were a perfect match.

Chelsea took a sociology seminar I offered in the fall of 2008. She had transferred to CCS after a few years working and taking classes in western Michigan. She sat in the second row each week. She rarely said a word in class. What I mostly remember about that semester is her brand-new pair of gray UGG knit boots. She wore them every week. And, without me knowing anything about her, those boots offered me some clue about her desire to be seen. That year, UGGs were all the rage. And the knit, fold-over, oversized-button style were ever so slightly fashion forward. Chels wore them each week with old jeans and T-shirts that looked as if they had been pulled from a Salvation Army neighborhood bin. There was something so endearing about her obvious effort to "fit in" with the other college students. For some reason, I saw those boots as a signifier for her determined and dignified care for herself. Over the years of our friendship this initial intuition proved to be correct.

One evening in class, I shared a dream I had had the night before. I honestly can't remember why I shared it. Perhaps I was just wasting time. Three hours of lecturing gets long. At any rate, at the midpoint of my retelling, Chelsea interrupted me and finished the story of the dream. To say it was bizarre is a bit of an understatement. The whole class sat in rather stunned silence for a moment or two. Then, we awkwardly moved on. After class, Chelsea and I shared a short laugh over our coincidental dream sequencing. And that was that. The semester ended, and we went our separate ways.

In fact, shortly after that semester, I took a year off from CCS to concentrate on other projects and my own growing children. In the fall of 2010, as a precursor to my proposed course "Consciousness, Creativity, and Identity," I decided to sponsor a few on-campus lectures about meditation. I needed to recruit some student interest and thought immediately of Chelsea. My only problem—I couldn't remember her name. I did, however, recall that she tutored in the student success center. I called the director, Arlene LeCours, and asked, "Arlene, do you happen to remember that girl with the long blond hair and tongue ring who always wore those gray knit UGGs?"

She exclaimed, "Chelsea? She literally just popped into the office for the first time this semester. I'll put her on the phone."

I invited Chelsea to attend that first crazy meditation meeting that ended in my fist-pounding chair yelling that meditation had no home in academia. A Hollywood A-list actor could not have done a better job inspiring Chelsea's naturally rebellious spirit. From that moment on, Chelsea became my partner in crime. She learned Transcendental Meditation a few weeks later.

My own journey with meditation had begun because my mother offered to pay for me to learn and to watch my two babies for the few hours of instruction. Frankly, I would have gone to have my fingernails pulled out for the couple hours of free babysitting. I wasn't all that interested in meditation. For the first five or so years of my practice, I closed my eyes, began repeating my mantra, and promptly feel asleep—head-bobbing, drool-inducing, heavy sleep. There was no magic "poof" moment of profound understanding. Meditation was just what I did in the late afternoon when my babies napped. It was a good way to get some shut-eye. This was not Chelsea's experience. Chelsea meditated one time and seemed utterly transformed. She opened her eyes after her first meditation and said, "Molly, every student needs to learn how to meditate. How are we going to make that happen?"

You know, if the truth be told all these years later, I think I was a bit intimidated by Chelsea's earnestness. She really believed that *I* could make this happen—for students everywhere. It was a tall order. Chelsea started recruiting students to take my class—which, by the way, had yet to be approved by the department. I warned her that we might not be successful getting the class approved. She smiled and said, "Of course we'll get it approved, it's my last semester." She miraculously found a way around the administrative resistance by having the chair of the film department suggest teaching it as an experimental class. And, as luck would have it, the resistant former chair of liberal arts left the department. My more open-minded friend, Michael Stone Richards, stepped up and approved the class to run in the winter of 2011.

It's honestly difficult to describe the emotions I felt teaching that semester. At risk of sounding too clichéd, everything took on a feeling of importance, resonance, and meaning. Each student felt familiar. The stories shared in class seemed to ping-pong off the walls and slam into our hearts. I would think to myself while in the process of lecturing, "How do I know all this stuff?" It was as if a new part of my life was unfolding right before my eyes in ways unexpected and surreal. Again at the risk of sounding clichéd, it truly felt magical.

Chelsea graduated in the spring. During her final semester, she made a seventeen-minute film, *Tuning the Student Mind*, documenting the process of putting the class together and making the call to action for classes just like it on other campuses. The film premiered at the student show that spring. I remember meeting Chelsea's parents that evening and feeling a bit envious of their life-long connection to this sweet, talented young woman. I knew the likelihood of our staying in touch was low. Chelsea left Detroit the week after graduation. True to form, she needed an adventure. When she drove off to Denver with her pet snake, I doubted she'd look back.

It was the following winter when I next heard from Chelsea. She called one snowy morning and said, "I just can't stop thinking about how much your class changed me. We've got to keep working together!" I couldn't imagine what we might do, but I wanted to support Chelsea in whatever way I could. After all, I owed her. I suggested she start a blog called Tuning the Student Mind. She could write short posts on meditation, healthy eating, and the environment (her true passion). I sent her a check to pay her for her time. And, once again, Chelsea forged ahead, stretching my ideas about what was possible. We'd check in once or twice a month and chat about how to get students involved in our efforts. Together, we wrote blog posts and tossed ideas back and forth. We chatted like old friends and laughed a lot about our dreams and hopes for the future of consciousness-centered education. Somehow, we just knew we were onto something very cool and inspiring.

About a year later, I bumped into an old friend of mine, Una Jackman, whom I had met in the waiting room of our daughters' Irish step dancing school. Una had recently produced a documentary film about the Joffrey Ballet that I had read about in the *New York Times*. We hadn't chatted in a long time, and she suggested we get together to catch up. The next part of this story is so over-the-top bizarre that I just have to tell it to you straight: Over lunch, I told Una about my work at CCS and Chelsea's short student thesis film. She said, "Molly, this is such a great story! You've got a film in the making. If I give Chelsea five thousand dollars, do you think she'd be interested in expanding her film and sharing it with others at Mountainfilm in Telluride next spring?" Well . . . maybe, she just might.

Initially, Chelsea and I figured the film would document the benefits of integrating meditation into the classroom by interviewing teachers from across the country. But it became obvious very quickly that there simply weren't that many consciousness-centered programs around. Chelsea decided the film needed to be about the transformational journey of students taking my class. While I felt immediately intrigued by this approach, my feelings about being filmed in the classroom were mixed. Our first attempts were hilarious. First off, the camera immediately rendered me tongue-tied and inarticulate. And, second, the B-roll (supplemental footage intercut with the main shot) revealed that my audience was less than enthusiastic—often barely awake or distracted by phones, friends, and wandering minds. We shared so many laughs watching the initial footage.

In the end, however, Chelsea persevered. She organized a Kickstarter campaign that raised just over $27,000 to complete the film. Our time in Telluride produced a relationship with the Creative Visions Organization in L.A. As part of their Creative Activist Partnership (CAP Program), we met some amazing people who helped us gain confidence and find connections. The film was completed in just over two years. It premiered at the Freep Film Festival in Detroit, later aired on Detroit Public Television, and was nominated for a Social Impact Media Award. I have shown it on dozens of college campuses as part of different speaking engagements. My sweet husband still cries every time Natasha says, "Molly Beauregard, you changed my life," during the graduation sequence.

I refer to the film as a love letter. It remains the sweetest gift I have ever been given. The film sparked the realization for me that teaching is art. Watching my students from the vantage point of film offered me this profound recognition. I always knew how much my relationships with students changed me. In fact, I repeatedly share with students that my teaching is a selfish endeavor. I like to hear myself talk. My best learning comes in the process of explaining to others what I know to be true. Interacting with students is where I find everything that has ever been lost to me—all the knowledge, the love, the sweetness of connection—the purity of knowing comes unbidden in the interactional grace of teaching. It is where I find myself. But, ironically I suppose, I had never guessed that my teaching impacted students to the same degree.

I have one more story about Chelsea to share. A few weeks before graduation, Chelsea just happened to tell me about her grandmother. Her grandmother was adopted as a baby. Her whole life she ached to find her biological parents. Given the time in which she was born, her birth records were sealed. Rather than feel defeated by her own personal disappointment, she worked tirelessly to change the laws in Michigan to support open adoption. In addition, over the course of about thirty years, she was personally responsible for reuniting over five thousand adopted children with their biological parents or siblings, or both. It was an inspiring story. There is no doubt that some of Chelsea's "get it done" spirit has been inherited from this woman.

Chelsea's grandmother did eventually discover her biological mother's name. Sadly, her mother had long since passed away. She did, however, find comfort in knowing her mother's name. Listening to Chelsea's story, my heart ached for her grandmother but rejoiced in knowing she had finally found some closure. Turns out, Chelsea's biological maternal great-grandmother was a woman named Mae Comerford. My own great-grandmother was named Mary Ellen Comerford.

While Chelsea and I are unaware of whether or not these two women were related, we just relish the coincidence. It confirms to both of us our meant-to-be friendship. When Chelsea graduated, I baked her a Bundt cake. In the center, I placed a little vase filled with spring flowers. The vase was her gift. This is a tradition handed down from my own great-grandmother. My connection with Chelsea confirms to me that over and over again, we find each other in different lives. A true love connection can never be broken. I am grateful beyond all description for finding Chelsea in the most unexpected and beautiful way.

Student E-mail:
Noah—What I'm Struggling to Find within Myself

Molly,

This is Noah from your class, I just wanted to email you and say I appreciated the lecture today. Ironically I had a discussion with my mother the other day, about similar things and it feels like there is something trying to make me understand what I'm struggling to find within myself (especially within the past week). And then before I left you thanked me, it was really motivational to hear that and I just wanted to thank you for your time today despite your personal endeavors. However I am also curious as to how you picked up on that energy or whatever you may describe it as. I know it's there, but I'm trying to understand it more. If you have time to expand on it that would be great. Again thanks for your time.

Best,

Noah

Ah, Noah,

Hm . . . sometimes the intangible is difficult to explain in tangible ways. Similar to describing the color green—describing a deep knowingness is tough. Here's what I can tell you: underneath the surface level, everything is not only connected with everything else but also to the deep, unmanifest aspect of life itself. There is really nothing magical about it. When you've meditated as long as I have, you start to grow a connection between the here and now and the infinite beyond. Your strong desire to hear/learn from my lecture literally helped to pull the knowledge right out of me. Simply put—it was our connection (your desire to know commingling with my desire to share) that inspired most of my lecture yesterday. That is why I thanked you as you left the class.

Hope that helps a bit . . . . . :)

Molly

Fourteenth Week

How Do We Create a More Compassionate World?

Disrupting a reality so pervasive that we can't see any other way of being is not possible without shedding the "old mind" conditioned by our culture. And it is precisely at this crossover between the reactive mode of deconstruction and the more active mode of reconstruction—in which we are no longer merely the observers of our social fate but are participating co-creators—that a change from old-paradigm dynamics into new is likely to occur. *As participating co-creators, we become ourselves the shapers of the new frameworks,* the orchestrators of culture and consciousness.

—Suzi Gablik

A Tragedy Averted

Sometimes, I have students who complain that they have no stories to share in their final papers. When I question them, it becomes quickly obvious that they believe in the kind of drama that rhymes with trauma. They doubt the legitimacy of their everyday stories.

When this happens, I share with them the story of a farmer living in Minnesota. He was using all kinds of chemicals on his land. One night he was giving his baby daughter a bath, and as he cupped the water in his hands to rinse her hair, he started to think about all the chemicals he knew had run off his land into the water. He knew he needed to find another way to grow his crops. He went to the town hall and shared that story. The people in that small town were horrified—as they had small baby girls and boys at home who they loved and would never dream of hurting. And, over time, that community worked together to find healthy alternatives to the harmful chemicals they had been using to farm their land.

To me, this is a story of what can be—a future where we live the tenets of Bellah's so-called social ecology. It is also a story about which stories we choose to tell, and how we choose to tell them. Think about it. The farmer's baby did not need to die before he became motivated to avert disaster. He simply needed to feel the love that coursed through his being in a quiet moment of connection, then to take action grounded in that love to make his community a better place.

Students need to understand the stories they have been told about themselves. And they need to be empowered to change those stories, to reframe how they interact with the world with a greater understanding of their power to play an active role in bringing about change rooted in compassion and love.

Stories for Change

Social change is a basic fact of life. Presidential elections shift power structures, companies go out of business, new ideas come to life in the form of medical breakthroughs and transformational technologies. Less dramatic changes impact individuals as well; shifts in a familiar landscape due to a building being torn down, moving to a new city, the birth of a baby. Confronted with new circumstance, humans adapt. We change our beliefs, our behavior, and eventually our institutions in ways that reflect changes.

But how many of us actually see ourselves as actors on the stage of social change, rather than extras in the background who never get to speak, shepherded from one spot to another by forces we scarcely understand, let alone control? We must educate young people to act with agency and awareness rather than allowing themselves to be buffeted and blindsided by the winds of change, unknowingly upholding institutions that perpetuate injustice and inequality. An education devoid of reflection, compassion, and connection will not create citizens who apply these qualities to shaping the world they inherit.

In his groundbreaking book, *Emotional Intelligence*, psychologist Daniel Goleman argues that qualities such as empathy, self-awareness, and relationship skills are important—and often overlooked—measures of intelligence.[1] Individuals who have emotional empathy and awareness are better able to understand different perspectives. This helps them to communicate more clearly because they are better able to read situations, be tolerant of other people, and manage their own emotions. While teaching these skills in the classroom is tricky, I believe it is not only possible, but imperative. And these are all skills my own students report growing after taking my class (see appendix).

As Daniel Barbezat and Mirabai Bush write in *Contemplative Practices in Higher Education*, "It is vital that we provide exercises and time for students to reflect on how the material in their courses affects and challenges their own sense of meaning. Along with guidance in this inquiry, students need to be supported in learning to attend to the implications and consequences of their actions; without an understanding of the impact our behavior has on ourselves and on others, we are destined to create harm and suffering."[2]

People do not always realize their own internal knowing because they are overwhelmed by the stresses of life. According to a 2018 report of the American College Health Association, more than 60 percent of college students said they had experienced "overwhelming anxiety" in the past year. Forty percent said they felt so depressed they had difficulty functioning.[3] Teaching individuals to free themselves of the stresses and strains that limit their ability to see themselves clearly is the greatest gift you can offer in the classroom. Meditating in class together helps to create an atmosphere of nonjudgment, compassion, and peacefulness. It ripens the space for true discovery. It opens the space for new stories. Compassionate classrooms bring the power of empathic understanding to life, which in turn leads to both individual and collective action directed toward creating a better world.

I started this book by posing a question: How do we teach students to see and understand our connections and the sameness that underlies all

---

1. Daniel Goleman, *Emotional Intelligence* (New York: Bantam, 1995).

2. Daniel P. Barbezat and Mirabai Bush, *Contemplative Practices in Higher Education: Powerful Methods to Transform Teaching and Learning* (San Francisco: Jossey-Bass, 2014), 200–201.

3. Brad Wolverton, "As Students Struggle with Stress and Depression, Colleges Act as Counselors," *New York Times*, February 21, 2019; https://www.nytimes.com/2019/02/21/education/learning/mental-health-counseling-on-campus.html.

our experience—our common humanity? My intention with this question is not to deny the validity of traditional identity studies pedagogies. In fact, I believe it is of paramount importance that we acknowledge the ways our race, class, gender, and social roles inform our waking, daily life. While I have not identified my students in this book through traditional identity paradigms, as I conclude, I think it is interesting to note that the student voices in the book include LGBTQ, straight, black, white, biracial, Asian, Hispanic, immigrant, men, women, abused, rich, and poor individuals. Semester after semester, I am amazed and delighted by the diversity of students I have the pleasure of getting to know. Veterans, foreign-born adoptees, autistic kids, cancer survivors, kids who hurt, and kids who dance—all young people who delight me with their curiosity, their stories, their insight, and their willingness to dive into new ways of knowing.

There's a reason I tell story after story in my class. There's a reason this book is full of so many stories, large and small. Human beings understand the world through stories. We use stories to share our experiences, perspectives, and feelings with other people. Helping students understand their stories in the broader context of community, we enhance both the personal and universal meaning of those stories. We can never truly know what it is like to be someone else, for even an instant. Listening to others recount their experiences of the world with an open heart is the closest we can come. By truly listening to each other's stories, my students learn to value each other as the complex, multifaceted individuals they are beneath the surface markers of identity, and this leads them to look at themselves in the same way.

There is a line in the *Tuning the Student Mind* film that always gets an audience reaction. It is when I say to a group of students, "You're perfect. And any aspect of you that feels less than that is an aspect that simply hasn't been fed in the right way." Students cry tears of relief when they hear this line. And faculty question me on how I can offer such a broad, overarching statement without evidence. My response to both groups remains the same: we are all perfect in our potential. When we try to understand ourselves solely on the surface level of our attributes, we miss the complete picture of our true nature.

The philosopher and educationalist John Dewey believed that in order to study life and education, one must first recognize the impact of experience. For Dewey, education is a social and interactive process where students should be encouraged to not only learn a predetermined set of skills but also how to live meaningfully in the world. Helping individuals reach their full potential, according to Dewey, requires teaching them how to contribute to the good of the whole. As Rudolf Steiner, another great educationalist, wrote, "The human individual is the source of earthly life. States and societies exit because they turn out to be the necessary consequence of individual life."[4] *The manifestation of creativity is the human lived experience.* The "world" as we know it exists through our experiences, our interactions, and our collective thinking.

What happens when we deny individuals the experience of sharing their perspective with others in an open and flexible environment? In my opinion, we create a closed-off and often defensive classroom atmosphere. Everyone retreats into feelings of judgment and misunderstanding. Invariably, in this type of atmosphere, we cut off nourishment to the heart.

Education should provide opportunities to see knowledge as unlimited and learning as nourishing for the heart and mind. True learning is grounded in the deeper experiences of the spirit. The spirit should not be regarded as the antithesis of critical reason but as the unfailing guide of critical reason. When intellectual life is supported by a deep intuition and contentment, its functioning becomes creative, fruitful, and significant instead of barren, ineffective, and meaningless. Exploring both subjective and objective ways of knowing invites students to connect with what moves them at the deepest level of awareness and encourages them to continue to seek knowledge beyond the confines of the classroom. When students embrace learning as the purpose of life, every experience become ripe with possibility. Even in our darkest hours, we see potential.

The Empowerment Plan

Years ago, in my "still yearning to be a hippie" days, I read an article in the *New York Times* about person-to-person peacemaking. I can distinctly remember my dismissive attitude. "What?," my twenty-eight-year-old mind screamed, "We gotta burn down the house!" The idea that tending to your own garden in the hopes that your neighbor might follow just didn't inspire much enthusiasm in me. I dreamed of large protests, collective action, and shaking my fist at the Man. Makes me laugh today.

---

4. Rudolf Steiner, *Intuitive Thinking as a Spiritual Path: A Philosophy of Freedom, Centennial Edition*, trans. Michael Lipson (Hudson, NY: Anthroposophic Press/Steiner Books, 1995), 161.

Over the years, I have slowly learned that solving problems by attacking them head-on is not the best strategy for success. The best way to create meaningful change is to build something better next to—or, if you are really sneaky, within—the problem. Attacking problems directly is akin to throwing gas on an already burning fire. The flames shoot up with increasing heat and defensive energy. Working quietly, diligently, and creatively is a far better plan of action. The greatest compliment I have ever received came from a student who, upon leaving the meditation instruction room, smiled slyly and gushed, "Gee, Molly, you're really a radical." Yup.

The ideas presented in this book are part of the emerging trend in higher education to include contemplative practices in the classroom. These practices lead students to acquire a kind of consciousness that, in turn, leads them to become aware of their personal values, which ultimately become the foundational platform required for compassionate action. Bringing together subjective, objective, and transcendent ways of knowing in the classroom, we encourage mindful reflection and choice making. Consciousness-centered education models intend to encourage pathways to develop peace both within yourself and the broader community in which you reside. The work of many of my former students shows the action-oriented consequences of how this philosophy plays out in the real world. One of the most straightforward examples is the work of my former student Veronika, whose success I found out about rather accidentally.

If there is one thing that I am a stickler on, it is class attendance. A few years ago, a former student signed up to take a second class with me. When she missed the first two weeks, I was surprised. A good student, Veronika knew about my "skipping class" pet peeve. Toward the end of the second week of the semester, I received a rather breathless apology email from a very obviously busy young woman. Veronika, it seems, had been otherwise occupied. She had been invited to speak at the United Nations regarding her burgeoning nonprofit organization, the Empowerment Plan.

The Empowerment Plan is a Detroit-based organization dedicated to serving the homeless community. They hire homeless women from local shelters to become full-time seamstresses making coats that transform into sleeping bags. Veronika designed the sleeping bag coat during her sophomore year at CCS. Her coats are distributed free of cost to homeless individuals.

Prior to founding the Empowerment Plan, Veronika was enrolled in a freshman seminar I taught. In her final paper, she wrote about her own metamorphosis and her awakening to the many realities of life. I remember the assignment specifically because she bound her paper between two pieces of wood. There was a hand-drawn vine running between the front and back cover of the "book." On it were a series of illustrated butterflies. It was beautiful.

I have occasionally thought about that paper while watching Veronika's meteoritic success from the sidelines. I believe that for every situation in our lives, there is a thought pattern that fuels our actions and maintains our focus. It was as if that final paper served as a blueprint for Veronika's future success. As a young woman just breaking free from a challenging childhood, she had a strong desire to be seen as "worthy." By giving worth to others, she ultimately imposed worth back upon herself.

In 2011, Veronika won an IDEA Gold Award from the Industrial Design Society of America. She is also the youngest recipient to be awarded the prestigious JFK New Frontier Award from the John F. Kennedy Foundation. In addition, she has spoken at various conferences and colleges, has a TED talk circulating, and has been featured in numerous magazines, news shows, and newspapers around the world.

While it may seem like individuals have very little ability to shift cultural patterns, Veronika's success proves that individuals are the only ones who can do the work. It is through transforming our own lives that we create and construct new realities for both ourselves and others whose lives we touch. We are creativity in action, and where our personal action meets social issues, we are able to produce new ways of seeing the world.

It has been a joy to watch Veronika's journey unfold. Having recently enjoyed a coffee date with Veronika, I can attest to the fact that she remains grounded, sincere, and committed to meaningful social change. She is a powerful game changer. She also serves as an example of the type of student that consciousness-centered education programs produce. Imagine the world we might live in if more students had the opportunity to meditate as a vehicle to heal through awakening—through love—love of self and love of others. Imagine the possibilities for positive change these students carry with them out into the world.

Student Paper: SOC 322—The Remix

Occasionally, at the end of the semester, I take a sentence or two from each of my student's final papers and remix them, weaving them together to form a cocreated narrative that includes every student's voice. We sit in a circle on the last day of class and read the collective remix. Inevitably, there are tears of genuine emotion as students hear their own words echoed, reflected, riffed upon, and juxtaposed with those of their peers.

Peeling back the layers of self can be an unsettling experience. We come by our pain honestly. As I tell my students, "Everyone does the best they can." They groan, shrug, and look away in doubt until I explain further: "People do the best they can—given what they know, understand, and can see in the world around them. No one wakes up in the morning and thinks, 'Now, today is the day I'm really going to mess stuff up!'"

One of my favorite experiences every semester is reading the notes I invariably get at the bottom of student papers. If I had a dime for every student who apologizes for how "strange," "crazy," or "different" they are, I would be a very rich lady. The inevitable plea typically goes something like this: "Molly, I recognize that my paper is very strange. I am different from other people as my inner experiences and knowingness do not match what I present to the world." Of course, I always anonymously share these anecdotes with classes, saying, "I have the privilege of knowing that every single one of you has a rich inner life!"

When we operate from a place of deep individual authenticity and share it with others, our collective voices become more than the sum of their parts. They help us to recognize our role in the amazing web of interactions that form the broader culture. We see ourselves reflected in the words of our peers, and we recognize our connection to each other and the world around us. The remix paper serves as a metaphor, helping my students to envision a future where self-aware individuals create a worldwide network of connections and actively participate in democratic processes to improve their lives and the lives of others. The stories from each individual are separated by space breaks to distinguish them.

When I asked my mother if she could think of any defining moments in my life, she replied, "Oh, God, Henry! Your whole life has been a defining moment!"

I do not think I am wise enough to define who I am yet.   When we are small the world seems like it could be endless, undiscovered, and incomprehensible.   The eyes of youth are wide as they absorb the fascinating magic that the world seems to offer. Words that could describe this time for me are beauty, nature, imagination, creation, empathy, and solitude.   I was a tender, lighthearted toddler enamored with every tiny flower, plant, and creature. I thought I could hear the trees.   I thought I was guided by fairies and I believed I was surrounded by magic.   I believed within my heart that my connection to nature was more real than anything else in my tiny world, and that beauty was what the world would offer me.

When growing up some of us are forced to grow too quickly, like the flower trying to reach the sun from the shade, stretching and contorting to find the light just out of reach.   My childhood was intense.   I use my parents more as a guide of what not to do. I was constantly being pushed and pressured regarding who I was at a very young age.   Having lower-class parents that didn't go to college is really what set the tone early on in my life.

My parents' divorce broke down whatever sense of self I had left.   I was only five when they divorced.   With the terrible conflict between my screaming parents going on, entering the world of middle school was utter hell.   I was left to take care of my brother every day after school. My brother would cry every single morning without fail, and sometimes in the afternoon and evening as well.

I sometimes do not understand some of my behaviors.   Even at a very early age I remember consciously thinking and caring about what others thought of me, and would find it embarrassing when other children I knew misbehaved in public.   I was never one to throw a tantrum or make a scene.   I get lost inside.   I shut myself down.   I criticize myself endlessly.

Knowing they were talking about me, I decided to listen in while inconspicuously chowing down on a sloppy joe at a nearby picnic table.

From a very young age, I attended more funerals than a child probably should.   Death became a familiar thing to me. Lying in bed at night, I think about what happens when you die? What happens to all of your ideas and thoughts? What happens to your consciousness?   Since a very young age, my mind has swirled in anxious rumination. I absolutely despised thinking about death, but I would think about it often; and because I had so much time to think about it, I was instantly confronted with the issue of the magnitude of no longer being able to think. I think this got to me the most, just the idea of nothingness.   I felt alone and hopeless.   It seemed that all school cared about was preparing me for work.   One good thing about going to a terrible school is that you bond with your fellow students.   My kindergarten teacher brought the puppet out as a treat just for me. I have remembered her kindness ever since and the ways it changed the way I felt about school.

At six years old, a car hit me.   After the surgery, I was in the hospital for a month. The body cast was miserable—itchy, hot, and more claustrophobic than you can possibly imagine. Having to relearn old skills was traumatic. The situation was miserable. I would never wish this type of pain and suffering on anyone. During my baseball season in eighth grade, I broke my ankle badly. Undergoing major surgery at such a young age impacted me in surprising ways. It made me a stronger and more understanding young adult. The accident matured me in some strange ways. It's hard to describe the journey in words. To be honest, it was three months of complete hell that I would never want to experience again. The emotional and physical pain even to this day is hard to describe. I thank my family for being there.

As I grew up in misery, I began my own pursuit of freedom and happiness from my situation. I watched movies, and these movies taught me things and empowered my mantra. I can't even remember why I was suspended from school, but I vividly remember being sent home early. Naturally my mother was hysterical. I come from a family full of love, but also from a family full of sadness. When the family flew there for my cousin's funeral, we reevaluated our lives. At times I felt like the ambassador to the family fuckup that I secretly understood in more ways than they assumed. As I watched the life support machine pump his lungs, it was clear he wasn't going to wake up. Because of these things, I am incredibly self-conscious person. It doesn't take much for me to feel guilty over something if someone questions my actions. Couldn't anyone else understand my loss, my turmoil?

I actually liked being different and interesting, even if it meant I was a bastard. I saw my father in a weakened state and it was very humbling for me. My father symbolizes strength and active know-how to me. I was reminded throughout the entire process that our physical bodies at times face powerful disease and negative energy. Our time here on this planet in our physical bodies is best spent in as healthy a way as possible. When people are stressed we become unaware and cannot expand our consciousness to experience our internal bliss.

Spending my adolescence in two different cultures helps me to have some understanding of both cultures, but at the same time, it makes me not fit completely in either of them. I always try to belong to a group or something. My father came to the United States when he was eighteen as an illegal immigrant. My mother left the only country that she had ever known with her entire family still in it. They didn't have a penny between them. It was a total of twenty-six months for male Koreans to perform military service. During this long time, I happened to think seriously about my country's history, and unification of one nation.   When I am classified into an ethnic group, I feel alienated from others. This brings me shame.   After several years, I have now learned to hide my origins from people until they know me as a person. I am not ashamed of where I am from; however, I do not wish for people to form preconceived notions of my hometown that clouds their notions of who I am, whether they be good or bad. The totality of who I feel I am is far more important than any one label.

Even at a young age I would go to races with my dad, and having no idea what was going on, how it was scored, who the drivers were, etc., I would just watch the shapes move around for hours on end. It was this fascination with motion that first created my love for a pencil and paper. When I first started drawing I was in another world.   I've built professional racecars and played in bands, crashed cars, and seen people die.   I am the guy that types your name on the jumbotron at Red Wings games, and I'm never allowed back to Rite-Aid of South Pasadena. All in all, a pretty fascinating two decades.   From then on I began to control the way I did things, I made it a point to make sure everything was structured, planned out, and organized because in my mind I believed through structure nothing bad could happen.

The fact that my dad is now a general surgeon, after he came from Cuba where everyone was telling him his dream of becoming a doctor would never be a reality, is quite possibly the most inspiring element of my life.   My family is extremely encouraging; being raised around my loving family, experiencing the joy, and learning how to wittily respond to their pranks has really molded me as a person.   I am so thankful I was able to make it through these events with all the support I had from my parents and my girlfriend and my friends, who were there to support me the whole way through.   I ended up having a lovely yet distant relationship with my siblings and grew to love my dad for everything he has done in life whether socially appropriate or not. I learned that having animosity toward him was only hurting me.   Along the pathway of life people have seemed to grace me with resources that in some cases have relevance immediately, while others may take time for me to truly realize their worth.

So, where does it start?   I have trouble pinpointing the sources that identify who I am on a deeper level because I have trouble even identifying what my own weird deeper nuances are.   The road to self-liberation begins by reevaluating one's personal morality based on internal beliefs uninfluenced by the flawed institutions of our past.   Today, we must not simply rely on the status quo but challenge it based on a personal analysis, as opposed to learned habits.   The only authority now comes from within.   Being able to recognize yourself with all your talents, and shortcomings for that matter, is the most beautiful thing people can learn to do. You have to embrace others as if they were you and yourself as if you are others.   I have learned to embrace myself for everything I am and for everything I am not, and in a few cases it is what I am not that makes me anything at all.   It's all about those experiences you love and treasure, but it is almost more about those experiences and memories that scarred you and shaped your whole world at the same time.   These negative and positive events are both parts of the same coin.   I have become who I am because of both nurturing and strife, not one without the other.   I would not appreciate the peace I experience now if it were not for the tribulations I have faced.   I am me, me is all I am.   No one has dealt with my issues or walked in my shoes, let alone knows what it's like to spend a day in my head. I believe within our culture we need to reassess what it means to be successful and what true happiness is.   I try my damnedest to get things done right no matter how menial the task. I guess what my dad really taught me was to take pride in my work, whether it be a huge art project, or just a smudged-up window at work that needs cleaning.

There is a difference between being alone and being lonely. I've heard my mom say it a dozen times throughout my life. Such a simple statement, yet its complexity lies in actually feeling the difference. It's even harder to believe when it's coming from someone who couldn't take her own advice.   During two years of dating, I had been both physically and emotionally abused on numerous occasions, locked in a bathroom the size of a closet for acting out, and told that if I try to leave he will come after me. I was his possession.   Though these defining moments within my past were devastating, the life we live as a family today was well worth the wait.

Each time a butterfly moves its wings, it generates wind. I just know that I have a small role in the world's play and that anything that should happen will happen.   I learned saxophone and guitar.   After earning my Eagle Scout badge in the fall of 2005, the fun had barely begun.   I was getting into something that I did not think would follow me the rest of my life. I was busted again.   My whole life I've had a confidence manifested as constant intuitive actions. I believe subconsciously my ideas have been validated by my faith in our collective perspective.   I take things people say or do and twist them out of proportion to create some-thing completely ridiculous.   I love terrible films that take themselves so seriously that it backfires and creates something completely ridiculous and trying to play it off with a straight face.   I enjoy looking at terrible art and finding horrible things on the internet. To put it simply, I like flaws.   I've accepted my flaws, and therefore, I am able to accept the flaws of others.   All I need to worry about is how to be me more every day.

So, who am I? My fate is not only wrapped up within myself, but in the lives of others as well; in a very deep way we are all connected. If I am not aware of this, then how can I be aware of myself and know my fate and inner truth?   After all, the most important ideal of my manifesto is love; it is the supreme of life.   It is a great mystery.   It's all so beautiful and terrifying.   We must now take back our youth, our bodies, the fire, the creativity, and the compassion in us that cannot be packaged and shelved. We must abandon our forged image and be true to ourselves.   As I look back, I notice each of the defining moments in my life played a big role in defining me and also played a role in my other stories, as if it was a cause and effect chain.   Each story is a reflection of me and fuel for the discovery of me.   Every moment in life goes on to influence other moments near and far in the future, every action I make has impact, and every decision is a crossroad.   Why am I here? Did I enjoy it all the time? No. Did it make me mentally strong? Yes. Did it make me a better person? Absolutely.

I find it strange that I decided at such a young age what I wanted to be and have managed to stay on the exact path with no real deviation.   I have started holding ceremonies in my room. I am really weird. I light candles. I burn incense.   I want to interact from that level of kindness and love and purity—I do not simply want disembodied moments of "Aha" to inform my awareness/knowingness but true consistency of grace. Is that too much to ask for?   All these realizations came from my ability and desire to objectively question the world around me, desire which was instilled in me from the bizarre philosophy books my father used to read to my brother and me when we were children. Turns out, just hearing certain things, even if we don't understand them to the full extent of their meaning, makes an impression on a young mind.

Just like I distilled my religion to its core, I generally also distill everything I learn.   I now look at a pile of wood and envision beautiful furniture being made from it while my father and brothers, for example, see it all in flames.   I see a tree as not just a tree, but as a sculpture of nature, something that breathes life, and feels our presence.   This thought process has been evolving since the day I realized my hands and mind could work together to create.

Beautiful things happen every day and you'll see this if your eyes are open.   The sound of the waves from the beach would instantly sooth anxiety and stress.   I looked up into the trees and became mesmerized as their leaves formed into wiggly cell shapes.   To me, putting trust in something not tangible was silly, but I liked the idea of ghosts.   So, no, I am not Catholic, but I am also not Jewish, Muslim, Buddhist, Taoist, Atheist, Agnostic, or anythingist for that matter.

In order to impact the collective, we must first remember to pursue our own happiness.

I suppose happiness is like Bigfoot—you always see him when you least expect to! It becomes an extension of yourself, it is a living, breathing beast you must painstakingly manage and feed, and you must earn your results and love the process.

The whole world sighed.

My entire life seems to be moving fast, and sometimes I feel like I am just along for the ride.   I fell in love with a girl along the way and our relationship taught me so much.   My desire to impact and affect the lives of others still continues to burn within me.   My inner butterfly is kicking to come out of her cocoon, partly because she doesn't want to leave, the walls are comfortable. Identity is extremely sensitive to change.   I am certainly a different person than I was a year ago, because I have a whole new set of experiences against which I can judge my present interactions.   I formulate a series of self-expectations based on these judgments, and it is these expectations that constitute my identity.   I feel like unless we embrace who we are now, we will be so full of regret that it will drive us insane.   The metaphoric thesis for my paper is "there is no time like the present."   I have come to notice my sadness is starting to lift, and my anger is starting to come to the surface.   I am releasing my inner pain and I am beginning to develop and grow at a very fast and intense pace. But I am okay with it.   I happily live it every day.   Above all, I know if it is worth doing, it is worth doing now.   No other time is more appropriate for the things that really matter.   I am no longer lonely when I am alone.

* * *

This has been cathartic . . . funny, I had never thought about that—how all communication and interaction is really just catharsis. Again, I am reminded that I am always just an audience of one and in that is the fullness of life.

Conclusion

Letter to the Reader

The aim of life is self-development. To realize one's nature perfectly—
that is what each of us is here for.

—Oscar Wilde

Dear Reader,

It feels only appropriate to end this book with a letter to you.
While we don't really "know" each other, the act of you reading
this book has connected us, and I want to offer some final
thoughts directly for you.

I distinctly remember the day I "caught" the idea to teach
my students to meditate. Like a soft cottonseed drifting through
space, the idea entered my mind unbidden. Immediately, my heart
warmed and my optimism spiked. I knew I'd "caught a goodie"
(an old adage of my grandfather's, which first referred to jumping
big waves in the ocean). Later, when so many people resisted
my inspired idea, I remember feeling so surprised. What seemed
so obvious to me clearly threatened so many. Even now, after
eight years of teaching my course successfully, there is a top-level
administrator at CCS who continues to publicly refer to my class
dismissively as "that yoga class."

I've thought a lot about why I encountered so much
resistance over the years. There is an old Japanese proverb that
says, "The nail that sticks up will be hammered down." My first

175

attempts to integrate meditation into the core curriculum of an academic course were admittedly clumsy. The "hammering" of being questioned about the academic validity of my proposed course forced me to develop a strong academic curriculum to encircle the meditation component. That, I think, has become the strength of this class.

The questions posed throughout this book are the same questions I ask of my students. This format of asking questions is born of my own curious nature. It seems to me that the greatest questions of our time revolve around issues of identity. Who do we want to be? How can we become better than the generations that came before us? What would the world look like if we all lived as our best possible selves?

In an essay written in 1961, renowned novelist and essayist James Baldwin wrote: "Though we do not wholly believe it yet, the interior life is a real life, and the intangible dreams of people have a tangible effect on the world."[1] Ironically—or perhaps prophetically—this line serves as the concluding sentence in an essay titled "The Discovery of What It Means to Be an American." Now, Baldwin is writing about the role of the writer in society. But his thoughts on identity resonate profoundly with the arguments put forth in this book. As he writes, "The time has come, God knows, for us to examine ourselves, but we can only do this if we are willing to free ourselves of the myth of America and try to find out what is really happening here."[2] You could say that in my class, I aim to give my students the tools to investigate "what is really happening here" in the deep, self-aware way that Baldwin advocates.

As discussed throughout this book, we understand our surroundings and our identities by way of communication patterns, interactions with others, and our personal perceptions of the subjective experience of everyday life. The cultural context becomes the defining backdrop to our own knowing. So, I suppose the final question of this book becomes: What happens

---

1. James Baldwin, *Nobody Knows My Name* (New York: Vintage, 1992), 12.

2. Baldwin, *Nobody Knows My Name*, 11.

when we can no longer easily interpret the backdrop of our lives? We live in fast-moving times. Navigating our frenzied, often chaotic, and always noisy days can be disorienting and anxiety producing. As a result, it seems to me that now is the time to teach individuals skills that, in addition to helping them to move beyond the old paradigms of the past, help them to transverse the modern world. Consciousness-centered educational programs encourage a new understanding of the power of *relatedness*—particularly the relationship between subjective, objective, and transcendent ways of knowing.

The curriculum developed in my class rests largely on the idea that education needs to include and engage the whole person, integrating silence and feeling with empirical analysis and encouraging students to reflect on all aspects of their lives, and to bring this holistic way of thinking to everything they encounter. Importantly, this curriculum also serves as an answer to Baldwin's call to wake up to the splendor of life's possibilities. Digging at and questioning the foundational platforms for our beliefs, our roles in society, and our potential, we may finally break open and expose the "hidden laws"—Baldwin's words—that actually govern our society.[3]

Despite the fact that change tends to happen over time, we all seek radical moments of transformation. Just as one walk on a treadmill will likely not lead to a ten-pound weight loss, one or two meditation sessions will not induce a spiritual awakening. That said, with persistence and consistence, it is possible to wake up to a new way of living. Becoming aware of the ways that the world reflects certain aspects of yourself begins to grow your connection to everyone and everything.

I have a recurring dream in which I discover a brand-new room in my house. It's a wonderful dream of sheer delight; there's something magical about stumbling into a new space in my old house. Writing this book has felt a bit like experiencing that dream in my waking life. I've been pleasantly surprised by how much this material continues to reveal to me. Sharing my stories

---

3. Baldwin, *Nobody Knows My Name*, 11.

on the page requires a certain discipline—a tightening, so to speak. It feels different than the more organic, free-flowing nature of a lecture. In moments of frustration or writer's block, I find myself calling forth my future reader in my mind's eye. Who are you, I wonder? What do you wish to hear from me? How might I grow our connection—which from this vantage point feels so amorphous, ineffable, and remote?

And then I remind myself that you, too, are me—out in the world tugging on your own strand of golden thread. We weave together.

With love,

Molly

P.S. In the moments just prior to this book going to print, I discovered that the Angel Museum has closed. It seems that after twenty years of a successful run, the museum became too expensive to operate. A large auction house was hired to sell off the collection. And so the angels are now scattered throughout the world. Feels somehow prophetic to me.

Appendix

Consciousness-Centered Education Programming:
Lessons from Five Years
of Quality Improvement Data

Molly Beauregard, MPA, MA, Lead Researcher

Elizabeth McQuillen, MEd, PhD, Data Analyst,
Wayne State College of Nursing

Emily Birchfield Shakibnia, MPH, Program Consultant

Introduction

My interest in consciousness-centered education sprung from my concern that students were not happy in my classroom. Over the course of several semesters, increasingly distracted, overwhelmed, and anxiety-ridden young people tugged at my heartstrings. As recounted in this book, evidence-based research on meditation validated my approach to integrating contemplative practices in the classroom.

This book offers personal reflections from over seven years of teaching this curriculum. The following section shares some hard data collected over this same period. It is my hope that this data-driven section will offer other educators a leg up in their own efforts to find support for innovative, consciousness-centered curriculum initiatives.

Methods

As explained in this book, my Consciousness, Creativity, and Identity course at the College for Creative Studies in Detroit, Michigan has been developed with the intention of providing consciousness-centered education programming for my students. In an effort to understand the effects and improve the quality of my course, I have traditionally had students evaluate their experience through self-reported surveys. A mixed methods approach is utilized in order to comprehensively capture student experiences and opinions of the meditation practice, in their own words.

To date, surveys have been conducted from the fall semester of 2012 through the winter semester of 2018. I did not conduct surveys during the Fall 2014–Fall 2015 semesters; rather, I was focused on organizing a new training sequence as I explored utilizing a different meditation style for the course. Given the evolving nature of my evaluation efforts, the surveys have developed and changed over time as I have homed in on what exactly I want to measure. For purposes of this appendix, I will refer to the different surveys and subsequent data as Phase 1 (Fall 2012–Winter 2014), Phase II (Winter 2016–Fall 2017), and Phase III (Winter 2018). Presurveys were distributed on the day of the meditation training, toward the beginning of the course, and postsurveys were distributed on the last day of the course (only data from the postsurveys were analyzed for this appendix). In all cases, students were verbally informed of the survey purpose, their ensured anonymity, and that there would be no academic impact, whatsoever, from the survey. Students who consented began the survey, and I remained present in the back of the classroom. Data were analyzed and written up by a data analyst at the Wayne State University College of Nursing with assistance from a consultant.

Phase I
Fall 2012–Winter 2014
Class size of 20–21 students (eighty-three sets of data)
Students learned Transcendental Meditation

In a twenty-three-item survey, students were asked to respond to a series of quantitative and qualitative questions regarding how they felt after starting their Transcendental Meditation practice, as well as any benefits that they had noticed due to their practice. The primary quantitative question was "Please tell us how you have felt since starting the Transcendental Meditation program" with answer statements such as "Happy,"

"Depressed," "Anxious," and "Hopeful." The answer statements were rated on a five-point Likert scale with response options of "Much More," "A Little More," "No Change," "A Little Less," and "Much Less." Students also responded to qualitative questions, including "Please describe in some detail any benefits you have experienced from Transcendental Meditation practice." Quantitative data were analyzed by transcribing the numerical correlations of each student's response (i.e., "Much More" = 5); responses were then combined to assess an overall average change in attitude or emotion of the entire group.

Phase II
Winter 2016–Fall 2017
Ninety-eight sets of data
Students learned Primordial Sound Meditation

In a four-part quantitative survey with forty-nine total items, students were asked to respond to questions regarding their emotions, feelings, and personality. Fourteen of the items asked about how often the student felt a particular emotion in the past four weeks, including questions such as "How often have you felt nervous and 'stressed'?" These items were rated on a five-point Likert scale ranging from "Never" to "Very Often." Twenty-one of the items asked students to make assessments about themselves, using a five-point Likert scale ranging from "Not like me at all" to "Very much like me." The remaining fourteen items asked students to respond to statements detailing how they felt in the past seven days, including statements like "I feel peaceful." These items were rated on a five-point Likert scale ranging from "Not at all" to "Very much." Data were analyzed using Cronbach's Alpha to assess the reliability of the instrument, as well as a Varimax component factor analysis. Variables that did not fall under a factor due to lack of sufficient correlation were removed from analysis. Missing data were excluded.

Phase III
Winter 2018
Twenty-six sets of data
Students learned Primordial Sound Meditation

In a nineteen-item survey, students were asked to respond to a series of quantitative and qualitative questions. Seven items were demographic questions, and the remainder assessed their emotions and feelings, their ability to connect with and successfully complete their coursework, and, finally, their experience with meditation. These included questions such as "In the past four weeks, how often were you able to complete and turn in the assignments for all of your classes on time?" and "Please circle the response that most accurately describes your feelings toward the following statements: Meditating makes me feel less stressed; Meditating helps me to succeed in school; Meditating helps me to be more tolerant." These were rated on four- or five-point Likert scales, depending on the question. Finally, students were asked to respond to qualitative questions including "What do you hope to gain from practicing meditation this semester?" and "Do you find it easier to meditate as a group or by yourself? Please describe your experiences." Data were analyzed using Wilcoxian Signed Rank and Kendall's Tau-b Tests.

Results

Phase I

Table 1

Overall Average Change in Self-Reported Emotions/Feelings n = 83	
TM Frequency	0.79
Happy	1.87
Down in the dumps	3.94
Faith in the future	1.86
Goal-directed	1.96
Tired	3.27
Purposeful	2.13
Anxious	3.73
Energetic	2.35
Annoyed	3.62
Hopeful	2.11

Nervous	3.62
Exhausted	3.64
Trouble sleeping	3.81
Bad tempered	3.84
Fatigued	3.59
Depressed	4.03
Sad	4.01
Optimistic	1.97
Weary	3.53
Angry	3.97

1 = Much More, 2 = A Little More,
3 = No Change, 4 = A Little Less,
5 = Much Less

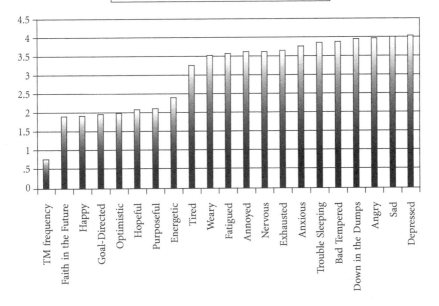

On average, all of the self-reported changes in feelings and emotions at the end of the semester indicated that students were experiencing positive benefits from the class, with some items yielding a more substantial change than others. Specifically, at the end of the course, students reported feeling much happier, optimistic, and more goal-directed; they also felt that they held much more faith in the future. Students reported the strongest change in feeling "more of" these emotions. Though these changes were not as large, they also reported feeling a little less depressed and sad (students reported the strongest change in feeling "less of" these two emotions), weary, fatigued, angry, down in the dumps, tired, anxious, annoyed, nervous, and exhausted. Finally, students reported that they had less trouble sleeping, felt more positive in temperament, and were a little more purposeful and energetic.

Students also provided statements that reflected their experience with and the benefits they felt from meditation that semester in more detail. While the extent of the benefits ranged among students across the four semesters, students were positive overall in their evaluation of how meditation practice and the course had impacted their general health and ability to succeed in their coursework.

Such statements included:

"Since learning TM I have felt much less stressed about home life as well as school life. After meditating I feel refreshed and the things that were stressing me out before seem much smaller and effect [sic] me much less."

"I have definitely noticed how much more focused/calm/aware I am when I do meditate and how drastically that changes when I don't. I make better choices, am more aware, kinder, more focused when I do. I am also more rested and calm."

"Meditation helps me to control my anxiety. I feel much more in control of my life and am able to not only quiet panic attacks more quickly, but also prevent them from happening altogether. Meditation has been one step in a new healthy lifestyle that also includes yoga, eating better, new sleep habits, and all around higher positivity. I am a better person because of this training and count myself blessed to have been able to be a part of this."

PHASE II

The Cronbach Alpha Reliability test revealed moderate to strong reliability for all sections of the survey, indicating acceptable reliability of the tool.

Table 2

Cronbach Alpha Reliability Results				
Survey Section	*Valid N Pre*	*Valid N Post*	*Pre-Test*	*Post-Test*
V1-V14	90	94	.822	.832
Grit 1-8	92	94	.740	.823
SW1-SW14	36	28	.824	.832
SC1-SC13	93	94	.773	.804

The Varimax component factor analysis revealed six factors that correlated most highly with one another: Peace, Difficulties, Meaning and Purpose, Diligence, Goals, and Comfort and Harmony.

Table 3

Change in Student Feelings/Emotions, n = 98		
Statement	Percentage of students who reported a change from pre-survey to post-survey (%)	Direction of change
PEACE		
I feel peaceful.	51*	Increase
I have trouble feeling peace of mind.	50*	Decrease
DIFFICULTIES		
How often have you felt that difficulties were piling up so high that you could not overcome them?	36	Decrease
MEANING AND PURPOSE		
I have a reason for living.	21	Increase
I feel a sense of purpose in my life.	31	Increase
I feel hopeful.	34	Increase
My life lacks meaning and purpose.	29	Decrease
DILIGENCE		
I am diligent.	22	Increase
I am a hard worker.	20	Increase
I am lazy.	27	Decrease
I wish I had more self-discipline.	34	Decrease

continued on next page

Table 3 (Continued)

Change in Student Feelings/Emotions, n = 98		
Statement	Percentage of students who reported a change from pre-survey to post-survey (%)	Direction of change
GOALS		
I often set a goal but later choose to pursue a different one.	31	Increase
New ideas and projects sometimes distract me from previous ones.	33	Decrease
I have been obsessed with a certain idea or project for a short time but later lost interest.	43	Decrease
I have trouble concentrating.	34	Decrease
COMFORT AND HARMONY		
I am able to reach down into myself for comfort.	49	Increase
I feel a sense of harmony within myself.	51	Increase
I find comfort in my faith or spiritual beliefs.	33	Increase
I feel connected to a higher power (or God).	25	Increase
*Significant at p<.001		

Peace

Students were significantly more likely to report positive changes in feelings of peace: 51 percent of the students reported an increase in feeling peaceful, with 50 percent of students reporting a decrease in having trouble feeling peace of mind.

Difficulties

Thirty-six percent of the students reported a decrease in the number of times that they felt difficulties were piling up on them; at the end of the course, students were also more apt (forty-one out of ninety-eight pairs) to report that setbacks did not discourage them.

Meaning and Purpose

Twenty-one percent of students reported an increase in feeling that they had a reason for living, while 31 percent reported an increase in feeling that they had a sense of purpose in life. Thirty-four percent of students reported an increase in feeling hopeful. Fewer students (29%) felt that their life lacked meaning and purpose.

Diligence

A small percentage of students reported an increase in feeling that they were diligent and hardworking (22% and 20%, respectively). Twenty-seven percent reported a decrease in feeling that they were lazy, and 34 percent of students reported a decrease in wishing that they had more self-discipline.

Goals

Thirty-one percent of students indicated in the postsurvey that they were more likely to set a goal and then later choose another one. More students reported being less apt to be distracted by new ideas and projects (33%). Forty-three percent of students reported a decrease in having an obsession with an idea/project but later losing interest. Thirty-four percent of students reported a decrease in having trouble concentrating.

Comfort and Harmony

Just under half the students reported an increase in whether they could reach down into themselves for comfort (49%). Fifty-one percent reported an increase in feeling a sense of harmony within. There was a smaller increase (33%) for those who found comfort in their faith or spiritual beliefs (with 47% staying the same), and 25 percent of students reported an increase in feeling a connection to a higher power.

PHASE III

Student Emotion and Feelings

Almost a quarter of the students (23%) reported that they came close to failing a course in the fall of 2017, and half of the students (50%) reported that they had seriously considered dropping out of college altogether. Students reported increased magnitudes of stress, anxiety, and feeling overwhelmed in the period of the postsurvey; they also reported increased magnitudes of disinterest in schoolwork, and in feeling disconnected from family. Students reported decreased magnitudes of being unable to think clearly, inability to control anger, and in feeling disconnected from other students, friends, and peers. In other words, at the end of the course, students felt that they did not have as much trouble thinking clearly or controlling their anger, and did not feel as disconnected to others as they had in the beginning of the course. At postsurvey, students were significantly more likely to report a decrease in their ability to complete and turn in their assignments on time.

Students' reported increase in stress was likely due to the timing of the postsurvey. In addition to finals, students were focused on end of year studio critiques. At CCS, this is an exceptionally stressful time, and it is expected that students would report greater stress during this period, compared to other times. This is perhaps one example of a threat to internal validity of the course model, known as "history." In this instance, external events (finals and studio critiques) occurred between the pre- and post-test. Such a threat can be controlled for, in the future, through improvements of the study design (by offering the post-test prior to the end of the semester.) Despite their inability to complete all their schoolwork, students did report feeling less stressed by their schedule. I propose a possible additional explanation for the increase in reported stress. After meditation, some students reported increased self-awareness. If students are more aware of their emotions and choices when meditating, they will notice more stress than they otherwise would, despite the stress being present regardless of meditation benefits.

Table 4

Student Emotion/Feelings in Past Four Weeks						
Feeling/Emotion	N of Pairs	Positive Differences	Negative Differences	Ties	Test Statistic	P Value
Have you felt stressed?	26	6	1	19	24.000	.059
Have you felt anxious?	26	8	2	16	44.000	.058
Have you felt overwhelmed?	24	7	4	13	40.500	.477
Have you felt depressed?*	24	5	5	14	32.500	.589
Have you felt unable to think clearly?*	24	5	9	10	42.000	.467
Have you felt disinterested in your schoolwork?	26	9	4	13	67.000	.106

Have you felt disconnected from other students?	26	4	6	16	20.500	.458
Have you felt disconnected from friends or peers?	26	7	9	10	65.600	.890
Have you felt disconnected from your family?	26	6	5	15	30.000	.776
Have you felt unable to tolerate the people around you?	26	9	5	12	63.000	.467
Have you felt unable to sleep like you normally do?	25	8	8	9	76.000	.668
Have you felt unable to control your anger?	26	3	7	16	20.000	.405
Felt able to stay in control of everything going on?	25	5	8	12	32.500	.317
Felt stressed or anxious about school work	26	7	4	15	54.000	.057
Able to complete and turn in assignments on time	26	1	13	12	6.500	.002**
Felt that assignments reflected best effort	26	4	7	15	22.000	.285

* Asymmetrical distribution of differences
** p<.05

Key: 1 = never, 2 = rarely, 3 = sometimes, 4 = often

Impact of Meditation

Students who reported a higher frequency of meditation were significantly more likely to report a decrease in feeling disconnected from other students, as well as in their inability to tolerate people around them; this means that the more a student meditated, the more likely they were to feel connected to and tolerant of students and other peers.

Table 5

Association Between Frequency of Meditation and Student Feelings/Emotions in Past 4 Weeks				
Feeling/Emotion	N of Valid Cases	Association Value	Approximate T[b]	Approximate Significance
Have you felt stressed	25	−.123	−.695	.487
Have you felt anxious	25	−.040	−.199	.842
Have you felt overwhelmed	24	−.147	−.782	.434
Have you felt depressed	25	−.017	−.014	.917
Have you been unable to think clearly	25	−.030	−.241	.810
Have you felt disinterested in your school work	25	−.093	−.603	.546
Have you felt disconnected from other students	25	−.342	−3.028	.002*
Have you felt disconnected from friends and peers	25	−.157	−1.562	.118
Have you felt disconnected from your family	25	−.175	−1.068	.285
Have you felt unable to tolerate people around you	25	−.377	−2.621	.009*
Have you been unable to sleep like you normally do	25	−.184	−1.096	.273
Have you felt unable to control your anger	25	−.294	−1.568	.117
*P<.05				

Though stress levels and coursework incompletion were high among students at the end of the course, the vast majority of students (over 75% for each statement) reported that they felt benefits of meditation; specifically, meditation helped students to feel less stressed, more in control, more creative, and more connected to their schoolwork.

Table 6

Self-Reported Impact of Meditation on Student		
Statement	Number of Students That Somewhat and Strongly Agree	% of Students That Somewhat and Strongly Agree
Helps me feel less stressed	22	84.6
Helps me feel more in control	21	80.8
Helps me feel more flexible	15	60.0
Helps me feel more tolerant	19	73.1
Helps me connect to schoolwork	20	76.9
Helps me to succeed in school	18	72.0
Helps me connect to other people	19	73.1
Helps me feel more creative	20	76.9

Group versus Solo Meditation

Of the twenty-six students who responded to the qualitative question regarding preference for group meditation or solo meditation, the vast majority of students (77%, n=20) responded that they preferred group meditation. Students elaborated on their preferences with such statements as:

"[Meditation] is easier for me in a group. At home, I tend to get distracted. When meditating with the group, it reminds me that human beings can remain quiet together. It is also a bit easier to hold myself to my word when I am around other people who are taking time out of their day in order to meditate too."

"I feel more motivated to meditate in a group than alone. When I'm alone, I get distracted and don't seem to stay with the meditation as long. When I am with the group, it feels like a shared experience—it's powerful."

"I find it a lot easier to meditate in a group. When I'm alone it's hard to get myself into the habit of meditation. When I *finally find the time to meditate, I become consumed with all the things I need to get done. When I meditate in class, I feel better because the atmosphere is calmer."*

Discussion

KEY FINDINGS

Data from all three phases of our survey evaluations indicate that students are experiencing positive benefits from engaging in meditation practice. These data suggest that consciousness-centered education programming may have the ability to help students improve their mental health, and ultimately their academic and career goals. Overall, students have reported being happier, more at peace, and better able to focus on their coursework at the end of the semester than they were when we started together. Students also reported that they were better able to handle problems that came their way, and showed a greater sense of self-confidence.

Though stress and anxiety levels actually increased in Phase III, students reported that meditation helped them to deal with these issues; this suggests that perhaps outside factors influenced students' stress and anxiety levels at the time of the postsurvey (e.g., it was around the same time as final exams or students were stressed about final grades). Data from Phase III also show that greater levels of self-reported meditation practice positively influenced students' levels of tolerance and their ability to connect with other students; this suggests that consciousness-centered education programming can play a role in unifying students on college campuses and promoting greater ties to community. Qualitative data show that students are interested in and eager to utilize meditation as a way to manage stress and anxiety, as well as extreme coursework demands. Importantly, students also showed a meaningful preference for meditating together as a group, in the classroom. Students acknowledged that the obstacles to a successful meditation practice felt easier to overcome when in a group setting; these obstacles included distractions, making the time to meditate, and feelings of isolation in solo meditation practice.

LIMITATIONS

As these end-of-course surveys were intended for me to see how my students were responding to the course (and adjust/improve due to the results), these results cannot be generalized to other populations; they have also not been peer reviewed. Similarly, given that this was not conducted in an experimental setting, we cannot presume any causation. The population size for Phase III was small (one class size), so results should be analyzed with caution. We did not quantitatively assess students' preference for meditation alone versus in the group classroom setting; however it will be assessed going forward as this is a key piece of consciousness-centered education programming. Finally, given my close relationship with many of my students, there is the possibility of the existence of social desirability bias, in which students responded more favorably on the survey than they might have truly felt, because they wanted to please me.

Recommendations

Current research on meditation among college students is focused primarily on a meditation practice that is offered in the form of a specific intervention or extracurricular course.[1] Consciousness-centered education programming presents an innovative opportunity by utilizing the evidence-based practice of meditation as *part of the structure of a college-level course.* As a pioneering program, this Tuning the Student Mind–sponsored consciousness-centered education holds amazing potential to increase graduation rates while improving the overall well-being of college students around the country. To be sure, meditation practiced in a group setting while in the classroom is a unique approach that will not be suitable to all kinds of students. Different methods of providing these opportunities should also be developed and considered in order to reach the greatest breadth of students possible. However, the overwhelming preference of my students for group meditation suggests that consciousness-centered education programming offers an appealing approach for many college students.

Utilizing research to analyze the associations between consciousness-centered education programming and mental health, engagement with coursework, and academic performance is essential for efforts aimed at improving overall student health. Our quality improvement data are a first step in demonstrating the impact that this type of program can have; rigorous research on the topic would be a great contribution to

---

1. M. D. Bamber and J. K. Schneider, "Mindfulness-Based Meditation to Decrease Stress and Anxiety in College Students: A Narrative Synthesis," *Educational Research Review* 18 (2016): 1–32.

the field, and will provide the evidence necessary to continue to develop consciousness-centered education programs as a way to improve student health and academic outcomes.

Recommendations for Further Reading

The books on this list are my tried and true classics: fourteen books that serve as a constant source of inspiration and ideas. I've left a few giants off this list, including Ralph Waldo Emerson, Maharishi Mahesh Yogi, and John Dewey. On a semester-to-semester basis, I find that students desire and require different approaches to my subject matter. Like most instructors, I am always on the hunt for new ideas. There is a certain fluidity to the process; certain classes inspire me to seek out new resources or to bring in texts I don't use every time. The books on this list serve as the foundational platform for the core curriculum of my course.

Barbezat, Daniel P., and Mirabai Bush. *Contemplative Practices in Higher Education: Powerful Methods to Transform Teaching and Learning.* San Francisco: Jossey-Bass, 2014.

Contemplation in higher education is a relatively new field of study. This well-researched book provides an overview of the current landscape of contemplative instruction and curriculum development as well as the philosophy that serves as justification for the inclusion of contemplative practices in the classroom. While Barbezat and Bush acknowledge that institutions of higher learning do a good job teaching analytical skills, they insist that these skills will be enhanced with the inclusion of reflection techniques in the classroom. Further, they promote connecting learning to real-life experiences, suggesting that students value course material more when they understand the relevance to their own lives. Their book serves as an introductory history of the use of contemplative practices into teaching, learning, and research.

Bellah, Robert N., Richard Madsen, William M. Sullivan, Ann Swindler, and Steven M. Tipton. *Habits of the Heart: Individualism and Commitment in American Life.* Berkeley: University of California Press, 1985.

My dog-eared copy of *Habits* serves as my trusty best friend in class. More relevant than ever thirty-three years after its publication, *Habits* is the sociological gift that keeps giving. This graceful book offers in-depth discussion of the meaning of private and public life in contemporary America. Every semester I find new gems of meaning hidden in its rich analysis. Undoubtedly my favorite book on a list of favorites, I believe it should be required reading for every college student in this country.

Chopra, Deepak. *The Book of Secrets: Unlocking the Hidden Dimensions of Your Life*. New York: Three Rivers Press, 2004.

The Book of Secrets is my favorite Chopra book. And that's saying something—by my count he has written more than eighty books! This book reminds the reader that it is in the exploration of the inner life that one finds true meaning. We all want to know the answers for "the riddles of love, death, and God, good and evil" (2). By offering both subtle hints and probing questions, Chopra leads the reader on a journey toward unlocking the mysteries of life.

Christakis, Nicholas A., and James H. Fowler. *Connected: The Surprising Power of Our Social Networks and How They Shape Our Lives*. New York: Little, Brown and Company, 2009.

Connected is a great, accessible read that advocates for understanding our social networks as a gateway to learning more about both our individual behavior and our society. The book explores the impact of social networks on everything from suicide to sexually transmitted diseases, from back pain to laughing disease (or hysteria). Christakis and Fowler's incredible use of story-oriented examples makes this book feel totally relevant and less intimidating than typical academic books. While the book does not discuss consciousness specifically, it does offer scientific validation for the notion that human thinking and emotions are contagious. Christakis and Fowler's explanation of network analysis research reveals the tricky ways our notions about health, politics, culture, and religion are embedded in our interactional connections.

Gablik, Suzi. *The Reenchantment of Art*. New York: Thames and Hudson, 1991.

I can open this book to any page and find the seeds for a great lecture contained in one meaty paragraph. Gablik's writing is well developed, thoughtful, and, best of all, action oriented. *The Reenchantment of Art* is one of those rare academic books that moves beyond diagnosis and into the realm of recommendation. Gablik defines and redefines the uses, potential, and promise of art. She advocates for heart-centered, soul-defining, communal work. This book is an inspiration for readers who care about the future of the world and the role of art in it.

Gaventa, John. *Power and Powerlessness: Quiescence and Rebellion in an Appalachian Valley.* Champaign: University of Illinois Press, 1980.

Reading this book during graduate school truly provided me with one of those huge "aha" moments. Gaventa's thought-provoking analysis of how power relationships shape our world helped me to understand why people seem to accept their lot in life rather than rebel against it. The interlocking dynamics of power relations work as a shaping force in culture. Our quiescence becomes a natural response given our belief in the legitimacy of the power structures themselves. The fact that Gaventa writes so compellingly and compassionately about a population I am familiar with (due to my own research work) only heightens the relevancy of this work for me.

Goffman, Erving. *The Presentation of Self in Everyday Life.* New York: Doubleday, 1959.

As evidenced by my in-class "Wizard of Oz" exercise, I tend to borrow quite a bit from this classic sociological text. Likening social interaction to the role-playing that goes on in the theater, Goffman offers such an accessible way to think about identity construction. Given Goffman's emphasis on the relationship between performance and life, I find this book lends itself well to conversations about authentic identity and choice-making.

Henslin, James M. *Down to Earth Sociology: Introductory Readings (14th Edition).* New York: Free Press, 2007.

I consider this edited collection of essays my best cheat sheet. I use this book almost every week as I prepare for class. It offers students a complete introduction to big ideas in sociology and a few good reminders for me of the breadth of sociological insights that I might choose from in any given week. A few of the chapters are mainstays on my syllabi, including Harry Gracey's "Kindergarten as Academic Boot Camp" and James M. Henslin's "Eating Your Friends Is the Hardest: The Survivors of the F-227."

hooks, bell. *Teaching to Transgress: Education as the Practice of Freedom.* New York: Routledge, 1994.

Writing compellingly about the crisis in education, hooks laments the fact that students generally do not want to learn and teachers too often do not want to teach. She calls for a renewal of the teaching profession, insisting that there must be a challenge and change to the way "everyone thinks about pedagogical process" (144). She advocates that we develop new ways of knowing and different strategies for the sharing of knowledge. She offers inspiration for teachers, like me, who are interested in transcending the narrow boundaries of race, class, and gender and threading together connections between all members of society as well as reinvestigating the role of emotion in critical thinking skills.

Lippard, Lucy R. *The Lure of the Local: Senses of Place in a Multicentered Society.* New York: New Press, 1987.

Reading *The Lure of the Local* feels a bit like putting together a thousand-piece puzzle with no image to copy. Just when you think you know how it's going to turn out, Lippard tosses in a surprising connection or a new idea. Offering a unique perspective on place and space, this comprehensive and complicated book sheds light on all the ways landscape affects our everyday, subjective experience.

Mills, C. Wright. *The Sociological Imagination.* Oxford: Oxford University Press, 1959.

Honestly, I think I had to teach introductory sociology for three or four years before I truly "got" this supposedly introductory book. To have a sociological imagination, one must be able to observe the world with a certain level of detachment. And while I'm not sure Mills would have said it just that way, developing a sociological perspective is akin to becoming what the spiritualists might call "awake." By utilizing our sociological imagination, we empower ourselves to not only "see" the forces that influence the patterns of our current social life but also to reimagine our future.

O'Reilly, Mary Rose. *The Peaceable Classroom.* Portsmouth, NH: Boynton/Cook, 1993.

In her classic teaching memoir, O'Reilly writes of her personal experience as an English teacher, sharing value-oriented connections between school and the world outside of class. She makes clear in her writing that the kind of environment fostered in individual classrooms influences students in profound and lasting ways. O'Reilly writes with humor and grace. She is unapologetically honest with her frustrations, her doubts, and her dreams. I cherish her book—I keep it, along with bell hooks's classic, on my desk in case I am in need of a reminder as to why I keep on going back for more.

Postman, Neil. *The Disappearance of Childhood.* New York: Random House, 1994.

Choosing my favorite Postman book feels a bit like being asked which child I like best. I like them all, and depending on my mood during any given day, my answer may change. Postman is a revolutionary—a radical thinker and brilliant social commentator. Postman's writing produces true "aha" moments in my class-room. Students are continually amazed by the prescient nature of his thoughts regarding the impact of technology and TV on culture. He is the best example I can offer of why reading cultural cues gives rise to an understanding of things to come. In the end, I've chosen *The Disappearance of Childhood*, as it sheds a light on the feelings of loss and emptiness that so many young people feel today.

Skolimowski, Henryk. *A Sacred Place to Dwell: Living with Reverence upon the Earth*. Rockport, MA: Element Books, 1993.

A man ahead of his time, Skolimowski is the father of eco-philosophy. He writes with great insight, humor, and compassion, begging his reader to wake up to the beauty of the world. Skolimowski and I are kindred spirits; he is unapologetically in love with life. I actually wrote Professor Skolimowski a fan letter a few years ago. The note he sent back is pinned proudly to my bulletin board.

Bibliography

Armstrong, Thomas. *The Myth of the A.D.D. Child: 50 Ways to Improve Your Child's Behavior and Attention Span without Drugs, Labels, or Coercion.* New York: Plume, 1997.

Astin, J. A. "Stress Reduction through Mindfulness Meditation: Effects on Psychological Symptomatology, Sense of Control, and Spiritual Experiences." *Psychotherapy and Psychosomatics* 66 (1997): 97–106.

Baldwin, James. *Nobody Knows My Name.* New York: Vintage, 1992.

Barbezat, Daniel P., and Mirabai Bush. *Contemplative Practices in Higher Education: Powerful Methods to Transform Teaching and Learning.* San Francisco: Jossey-Bass, 2014.

Baudrillard, Jean. "The Ecstasy of Communication." In *The Anti-Aesthetic: Essays on Postmodern Culture,* edited by Hal Foster. New York: New Press, 1998.

Bellah, Robert N., Richard Madsen, William M. Sullivan, Ann Swindler, and Steven M. Tipton. *Habits of the Heart: Individualism and Commitment in American Life.* Berkeley: University of California Press, 1985.

Berger, Peter L., and Thomas Luckmann. *The Social Construction of Reality: A Treatise in the Sociology of Knowledge.* New York: Anchor Books, 1966.

Bruce, Gregor. "Definition of Terrorism—Social and Political Effects." *Journal of Military and Veterans' Health* 21, no. 2 (2013): 26–30.

Burke, A. "Comparing Individual Preferences for Four Meditation Techniques: Zen, Vipassana (Mindfulness), Qigong, and Mantra." *EXPLORE* 8, no. 4 (2012): 237–42.

Castaneda, Carlos. *Tales of Power.* New York: Washington Square Press, 1991.

Chang, Vicky Y., Oxana Palesh, Rebecca Caldwell, Nathan Glasgow, Mark Abramson, Frederic Luskin, Michelle Gill, Adam Burke, and Cheryl Koopman. "The Effects of a Mindfulness-Based Stress Reduction Program on Stress, Mindfulness Self-Efficacy, and Positive States of Mind." *Stress Health* 20 (2004): 141–47.

Chopra, Deepak. *The Book of Secrets.* London: Ebury Publishing, 2009.

Chopra, Deepak, and Rudolph E. Tanzi. *Super Brain: Unleashing the Explosive Power of Your Mind to Maximize Health, Happiness, and Spiritual Well-Being.* New York: Harmony Books, 2012.

Christakis, Nicholas A., and James H. Fowler. *Connected: The Surprising Power of Our Social Networks and How They Shape Our Lives—How Your Friends' Friends' Friends Affect Everything You Feel, Think, and Do.* New York: Little, Brown, 2011.

Condon, Paul, Gaelle Desbordes, Willa Miller, and David Desteno. "Meditation Increases Compassionate Responses to Suffering." *Association for Psychological Science* (2013). doi:10.1177/0956797613485603.

Cranson, Robert W., David W. Orme-Jonson, Jayne Gackenbach, Michael C. Dillbeck, Christopher H. Jones, and Charles N. Alexander. "Transcendental Meditation and Improved Performance on Intelligence-Related Measures: A Longitudinal Study." *Personality and Individual Differences* 12 (1991): 1105–16.

Crissman, Henry. "The Mobile Anagama." Henry Crissman's website. Accessed October 18, 2018. https://www.henrycrissman.com/the-mobile-anagama/.

Dalai Lama. *The Path to Enlightenment.* Translated and edited by Glenn H. Mullin. Boulder, CO: Shambala, 1994.

Delany, Samuel R. *Dhalgren.* New York: Bantam Books, 1975.

Doidge, Norman, M.D. *The Brain Changes Itself: Stories of Personal Triumph from the Frontiers of Brain Science.* London: Penguin, 2007.

Eagan, K., E. B. Stolzenberg, J. J. Ramirez, M. C. Aragon, R. S. Suchard, and S. Hurtado. "The American Freshman: National Norms Fall 2014." *Higher Education Research Institute* (2015), http://www.heri. ucla.edu/tfsPublications. php.

Emerson, Ralph Waldo. *The Spiritual Emerson.* London: Penguin, 2008.

Eppley, K. R., A. I. Abrams, and J. Shear. "Differential Effects of Relaxation Techniques on Trait Anxiety: A Meta-Analysis." *Journal of Clinical Psychology* 45 (1989): 957–74.

Frank, Anne. *The Diary of a Young Girl Anne: The Definitive Edition.* Edited by Otto H. Frank and Mirjam Pressler. Translated by Susan Massoty. New York: Anchor Books, 1990.

Gablik, Suzi. *The Reenchantment of Art.* New York: Thames and Hudson, 1992.

Gallagher, John. *Reimagining Detroit: Opportunities for Redefining an American City.* Detroit: Wayne State University Press, 2010.

Gaventa, John. *Power and Powerlessness: Quiescence and Rebellion in an Appalachian Valley.* Champaign: University of Illinois Press, 1982.

Girard, René. *A Theater of Envy: William Shakespeare.* South Bend, IN: St. Augustine's Press, 1991.

Goffman, Erving. *The Presentation of Self in Everyday Life.* New York: Doubleday, 1959.

Goleman, Daniel. *Emotional Intelligence.* New York: Bantam, 1995.

Gracey, Harry L. "Kindergarten as Academic Boot Camp." In *Sociology: A Down-to-Earth Approach, 12th Edition.* Edited by James M. Henslin. London: Pearson, 2013.

Greenleaf, Robert K. *Servant Leadership: A Journey into the Nature of Legitimate Power and Greatness.* Mahwah, NJ: Paulist Press, 1983.

Hanover, M. D. "American College Health Association–National College Health Assessment II: Undergraduate Reference Group Executive Summary Spring 2012." American College Health Association, 2012. http://www.acha-ncha.org/docs/ACHA-NCHA-II_UNDERGRAD_ReferenceGroup_ExecutiveSummary_Spring2012.pdf.

Healthy Minds Network. "Healthy Minds Study." Ann Arbor: University of Michigan, 2012. http://wwwhealthymindsnetwork.org.

Henson, Jim. *It's Not Easy Being Green: And Other Things to Consider.* Glendale, CA: Kingswell, 2005.

Hölzel, B. K., J. Carmody, M. Vangel, C. Congleton, S. M. Yerramsetti, T. Gard, and S. W. Lazar. "Mindfulness Practice Leads to Increases in Regional Brain Matter Density." *Psychiatry Research* 191, no. 1 (2011): 36–43. doi:10.1016/j.psychresns.2010.08.006.

Kabat-Zinn, Jon. *Full Catastrophe Living: Using the Wisdom of Your Body and Mind to Face Stress, Pain, and Illness.* New York: Delacourt Press, 2005.

Kabat-Zinn, Jon, L. Lipworth, and R. Burney. "The Clinical Use of Mindfulness Meditation for the Self-Regulation of Chronic Pain." *Journal of Behavioral Medicine* 8 (1985): 163–90.

Kelly, Joe. *Superman: What's So Funny about Truth, Justice, and the American Way?* Action Comics Volume 1 #775. New York: DC Comics, 2001.

Kinkaid, Tyler. "College Freshmen Are More Depressed and Alone Than Ever." *Huffington Post*, February 5, 2015, http://www.huffingtonpost.com/2015/02/05/college-students-depressed-ucla_n_6624012.html.

Laski, Marghanita. *Ecstasy: A Study of Some Secular and Religious Experiences.* London: Cresset, 1965.

Lim, D., P. Condon, and D. De Steno. "Mindfulness and Compassion: An Examination of Mechanism and Scalability." *PLoS ONE* 10, no. 2 (2015): doi:10.1371/journal.pone.0118221.

Lippard, Lucy. *The Lure of the Local: Senses of Place in a Multicentered Society.* New York: New Press, 1998.

Maharishi Mahesh Yogi. *Bhagavad-Gita: Chapter 7.* Vlodrop, Netherlands: Maharishi Vedic University, 2009.

Mannheim, Karl. *Ideology and Utopia: An Introduction to the Sociology of Knowledge.* Eastford, CT: Martino Fine Books, 2015.

Maslow, Abraham H., Bertha G. Maslow, and Henry Geiger. *The Farthest Reaches of Human Nature.* London: Penguin/Arkana, 1993.

Mayer, Elizabeth Lloyd. *Extraordinary Knowing: Science, Skepticism, and the Inexplicable Powers of the Human Mind.* New York: Bantam Books, 2007.

Mayer, John. "Waiting on the World to Change." *Continuum*. Aware/Columbia Records, 2006.

Miller, Henry. *The Wisdom of the Heart*. New York: New Directions, 1960.

Mills, C. Wright. *The Sociological Imagination*. Oxford: Oxford University Press, 1959.

Nagel, Thomas. *Mind and Cosmos: Why the Materialist Neo-Darwinian Conception of Nature Is Almost Certainly False*. Oxford: Oxford University Press, 2012.

Nagel, Thomas. "What Is it Like to Be a Bat?" *Philosophical Review* 84, no. 4 (October 1974): 435–50. doi:10.2307/2183914.

Nidich, Stanford I., Maxwell V. Rainforth, David A. F. Haaga, John Hagelin, John W. Salerno, Fred Travis, Melissa Tanner, Carolyn Gaylord-King, Sarina Grosswald, and Robert H. Schneider. "A Randomized Control Trial on Effects of the Transcendental Meditation Program on Blood Pressure, Psychological Distress, and Coping in Young Adults." *American Journal of Hypertension* 22, no. 12 (2009): 1326–31. doi:10.1038/ajh.2009.184.

O'Reilly, Mary Rose. *The Peaceable Classroom*. Portsmouth, NH: Boynton/Cook, 1993.

Ritzer, George. *The McDonaldization of Society*. Thousand Oaks, CA: SAGE/Pine Forge Press, 1993.

Rumi. *The Essential Rumi*. Translated by Coleman Barks with John Moyne. New York: Harper Collins, 1995.

Russo, Richard. *Straight Man*. New York: Vintage, 1998.

Shakespeare, William. *As You Like It*. New York: Penguin, 2000.

Skolimowski, Henryk. *A Sacred Place to Dwell: Living with Reverence upon the Earth*. Rockport, MA: Element Books, 1993.

So, K. T., and David W. Orme-Johnson. "Three Randomized Experiments on the Longitudinal Effects of the Transcendental Meditation Technique on Cognition." *Intelligence* 29 (2001): 419–40.

Steiner, Rudolf. *Intuitive Thinking as a Spiritual Path: A Philosophy of Freedom, Centennial Edition*. Translated by Michael Lipson. Hudson, NY: Anthroposophic Press/Steiner Books, 1995.

Stoykova, Katerina. *Bird on a Window Sill*. Lexington, KY: Accents Publishing, 2018.

Substance Abuse and Mental Health Services Administration, Center for Behavioral Health Statistics and Quality. "Results from the 2012 National Survey on Drug Use and Health (NSDUH): Mental Health Detailed Tables." 2013. http://www.samhsa.gov/data/NSDUH/2k12MH_FindingsandDetTables/ MHDT/NSDUH MHDetTabsLOTSect1pe2012.htm.

Susman, Joan. "Disability, Stigma Deviance." *Social Science & Medicine* 38, no. 1 (January 1994): 15–22. doi: https://doi.org/10.1016/0277-9536(94)90295-X.

Tocqueville, Alexis de. *Democracy in America*. Translated by Harvey C. Mansfield and Delba Winthrop. Chicago: University of Chicago Press, 2002.

Trama, S., and N. Cheema. "Transcendental Meditation: Nature and Perspectives." *Indian Journal of Health and Wellbeing* 7, no. 9 (2016): 928–33.

UNESCO Office of International Standards and Legal Affairs. "Declaration of Principles on Tolerance." UNESCO website, November 1995. http://portal.unesco.org/en/ev.php-URL_ID=13175&URL_DO=DO_TOPIC&URL_SECTION=201.html.

The Upanishads. Translated by Alistair Shearer and Peter Russel. Emeryville, CA: Potter/TenSpeed/Harmony, 2010.

Whitehead, Charles. "Six Keynote Papers on Consciousness with Some Comments on Their Social Implications: TSC Conference, Hong Kong, 10–14 June 2009." *Journal of Consciousness Studies* 17 (2010).

Williams, Raymond. "Advertising: The Magic System." In *Media Studies: A Reader*, edited by Paul Marris and Sue Thornham. Edinburgh: Edinburgh University Press, 1999.

Wilbur, Ken. *The Essential Ken Wilber: An Introductory Reader.* Boston: Shambhala, 1998.

Wilson, Edward O. *The Meaning of Human Existence.* New York: Liveright Publishing, 2014.

Wolverton, Brad. "As Students Struggle with Stress and Depression, Colleges Act as Counselors." *New York Times*, February 21, 2019, https://www.nytimes.com/2019/02/21/education/learning/mental-health-counseling-on-campus.html.

Wu, L. T., D. J. Pilowsky, W. E. Schlenger, and D. Hasin. "Alcohol Use Disorders and the Use of Treatment Services among College-Age Young Adults." *Psychiatric Services* 58, no. 2 (February 2007): 192–200.